More Memories

of

Nottingham

Edited by Geoffrey Oldfield

The publishers would like to thank the following companies for their support in the production of this book

Main Sponsor

T Hammond & Sons Limited

Bratts Ladders

British Geological Survey

Cooper & Berry Limited

Hopewell Limited

Imperial Tobacco

Leivers Brothers Limited

Nottingham Building Society

RJ Pickford (Electrical) Limited

Progressive Printers (Nottingham)

FG Skerritt

Speedo International

WC Wicks

Willoughby Garages

John E Wright & Company Limited

First published in Great Britain by True North Books Limited
England
HX5 9AE
Telephone: 01422 377977
© **True North Books Limited 2000**

ISBN 1 903204 11 9

Text, design and origination by True North Books Limited
Printed and bound by The Amadeus Press Limited

Nottingham - from strength to strength

The 20th century was a time of tremendous change all over Britain. In many cases, these changes came about as either a direct or an indirect result of scientific and technical advances. We began the century with horse-drawn trams; barely 50 years later, the trend which was to turn us into a nation of car owners was already perceptible. This, of course, had implication for city centres, and Nottingham adapted itself accordingly, creating dual carriageways for the traffic and paved areas for the pedestrians. Television played a major part in bringing to the fore a culture of consumerism, which in turn led to the creation of two major

shopping centres in Nottingham. Earlier, the city's retail trade had been dominated by long-established, local family business like Pearsons, Skinner and Rook, Griffin and Spalding, Farmers the drapers, and of course Boots. Television also influenced the nation's entertainment habits. Nottingham has a long tradition of providing splendid buildings where its citizens can enjoy their leisure, and although some, such as the Empire Theatre and the Hippodrome cinema, have been lost, others have survived, notably the Theatre Royal; built in the 1860s, this fine building has looked better than ever since major renovations were carried out in the 1960s.

Some parts of the city, such as Milton Street and Broad Marsh, the latter a Victorian slum, have changed beyond recognition. Others have evolved more gradually, adapting themselves more easily to the demands of 21st century life. Landmarks which came and went in the course of the 20th century included the grand Victoria Station; sadly, a number of cherished streets and buildings, including the Black Boy Hotel, had to be sacrificed in the name of progress. Nottingham escaped the worst of the the unemployment crises which caused great suffering in other parts of the country, and the three names which dominated the local economy virtually throughout the century were Raleigh, Players and Boots. Each of these manufacturing concerns was founded in Nottingham, and was built up by one man.

Raleigh went on to become part of a multinational organisation and is still a major employer; Players became part of Imperial Tobacco and has moved its former factories at Radford to new premises on the edge of the city. The Boots business has gone from strength to strength, and the city has benefited in a number of ways from what D H Lawrence, Nottingham's most famous son, once referred to as 'the noble loot Derived from shrewd cash-chemistry By good Sir Jesse Boot.' We hope that this collection of photographs will bring back memories for readers who lived through these years of change, while for those too young to remember they will offer an insight into what life was like for their parents, grandparents and great-grandparents.

Contents

Around the city centre

Traffic was more picturesque in 1929. Next to the Milton's Head Hotel - a very different kind of structure to the Victoria Centre which took its place - we can see Atkey's breakdown truck, waiting to emerge from Milton Street into Lower Parliament Street. A R Atkey had a motor spare parts warehouse in Trent Street. What, we wonder, would the mechanic of those days have made of the 21st century garage, equipped with all manner of hi-tech electronic diagnostic equipment. What, for that matter, would the average shopper of 1929 have made

of a state-of-the-art 21st century shopping centre? Within a relatively short space of time, one generation is taking for granted things which its grandparents' generation never even dreamed of. By 1972, Nottingham's new Victoria Shopping Centre stretched along Lower Parliament from Milton Street to Newcastle Street. Further along, between Newcastle Street and Glasshouse Street, two of the old buildings survived until the end of the 20th century: the building dated 1901 which became Argos, and its neighbour, the former gas and electricity showroom.

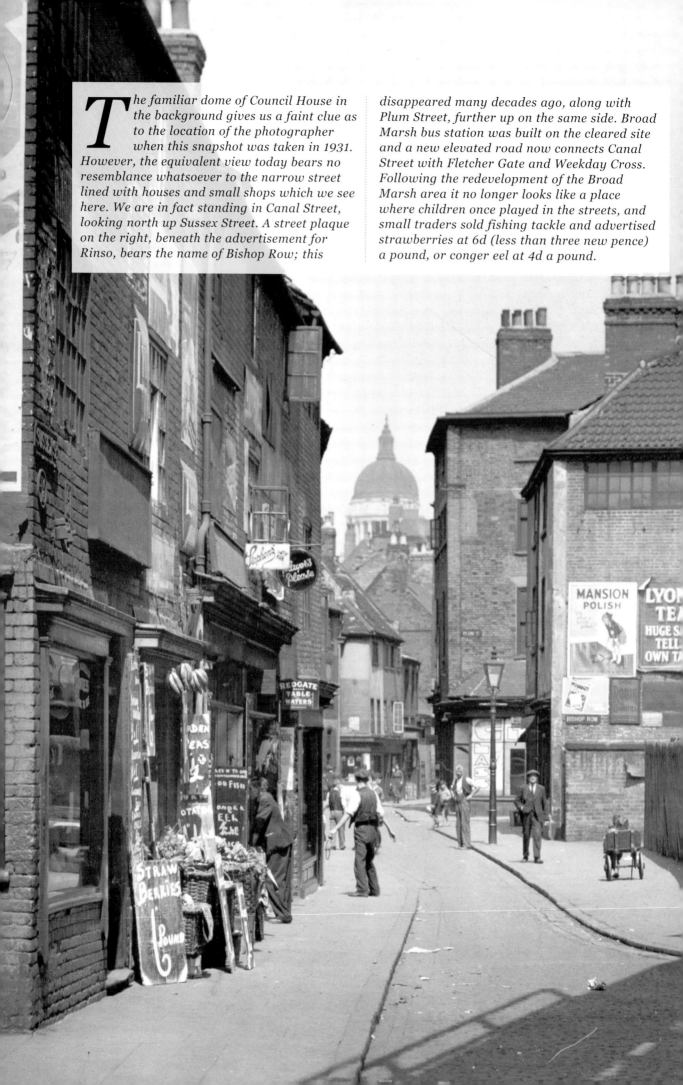

The familiar dome of Council House in the background gives us a faint clue as to the location of the photographer when this snapshot was taken in 1931. However, the equivalent view today bears no resemblance whatsoever to the narrow street lined with houses and small shops which we see here. We are in fact standing in Canal Street, looking north up Sussex Street. A street plaque on the right, beneath the advertisement for Rinso, bears the name of Bishop Row; this disappeared many decades ago, along with Plum Street, further up on the same side. Broad Marsh bus station was built on the cleared site and a new elevated road now connects Canal Street with Fletcher Gate and Weekday Cross. Following the redevelopment of the Broad Marsh area it no longer looks like a place where children once played in the streets, and small traders sold fishing tackle and advertised strawberries at 6d (less than three new pence) a pound, or conger eel at 4d a pound.

would be far better off in the Arboretum. So in 1927 arrangements were made to move him. He left Theatre Square, but he never took up residence in the Arboretum, due to an accident which befell him in transit. Surely nobody still bore a grudge from 1865 ...

Top: Nottingham's entertainment scene in the early 20th century included the Theatre Royal, the Empire Variety Theatre, the Hippodrome, the Elite cinema, the Elizabeth rooms above the Co-op in Parliament Street, and the Talbot, later Yates Wine Lodge. The Palais de Danse joined the ranks in 1925. This impressive building, with its Corinthian columns, its bronze frieze of dancing figures, and its ostentatious roof-top globe which later disappeared, to be replaced by a different globe in more recent times, was erected on the site once occupied by the House of Correction.

Above: In September 1908, the Hippodrome Theatre of Varieties took the place of Whitehall's factory, which burned down three years earlier. The Hippodrome was originally a music hall with a seating capacity of 2,500. Later, when cinema overtook variety and music hall in the popularity stakes, the Hippodrome was converted into the Gaumont cinema, which it remained until 1971. This photograph was taken in 1927, after the disappearance of a once-familiar landmark in Theatre Square. For almost 40 years a statue of Samuel Morley had stood in the road opposite the entrance to the Theatre Royal. Mr Morley was elected Liberal MP for Nottingham in 1865, but was subsequently unseated when it was revealed that some of his supporters had indulged in bribery and corruption during his campaign. This was quite a blow for the strict and upstanding Congregationalist. His statue, however, was brought down from its pedestal for a much more prosaic reason: as the amount of traffic through the square increased, it was felt that the gentleman stood in a rather inconvenient place, and

The glittering interior was as extravagant as the outside. In the centre of the immense dance floor, which could accommodate 800 dancers, was an 18 feet high fountain illuminated by changing coloured lights. Not surprisingly, the Palais was a tremendous success. Originally envisaged as a ballroom dancing club, it held regular tea dances for many years, as advertised on this 1930 photograph. Ladies and gentlemen could hire a professional 'sixpenny' dance partner, while ladies who had brought their own partner, and felt he needed sprucing up, could send him into the gentlemen's cloakroom for a shave and a shoe shine, or even to have the sharp crease pressed back into his trousers. The Palais' first resident band was Sid Reubens and his Savannah Band, and many well-known dance bands played there, Billy Cotton among them. When popular tastes changed the Palais adapted accordingly, becoming a rock and roll dance hall in the 1950s, and later a nightclub, known as Ritzys. Due to popular demand it has been given its old name, The Palais, but without the 'de Danse'.

Horse-drawn conveyances, motorised vehicles and bicycles create a scene of traffic congestion, 1920s-style. Wheeler Gate is pictured here in 1929. In the foreground to the right, the Canadian Fur Company is occupying a prominent position, reminding us of how attitudes changed during the course of the 20th century. People were not more callous in 1929; they simply had different priorities, and keeping warm was one of them. Homes were not centrally heated, travelling - as we can see from this photograph - could be a cold business, very

different from the warm, well-insulated cars which were to become the norm later in the century, and man-made thermal fibres were not developed to any extent until after the second world war. So a fur coat was the best way to keep warm. Readers may also remember the fur stoles which were popular in Victorian times and even later; often these came complete with the animal's head and paws, and though the idea of having the muzzle of a dead fox dangling down over one's bosom is likely to make the younger generation shudder, these used to be considered the height of fashion.

Above: Donald Wolfit and Rosalind Iden, whose names are splashed across the publicity banners in this photograph from 1966, were no strangers to Nottingham's Theatre Royal. Wolfit was a notoriously hard-working actor-manager who toured constantly with his own company and did a great deal to popularise the plays of the Bard. Born in Newark, he became one of the acclaimed Shakespearian actors of the mid-20th century, famous for his fine, resonant voice and his theatrical presence. In 1948 he married his leading lady Rosalind Iden, and as husband and wife they returned to the Theatre Royal later that same year. On that occasion they appeared in Ibsen's play The Master Builder. Theatre-goers old enough to remember Wolfit will no doubt have their own recollections of the many powerful performances which he delivered at the Theatre Royal, creating some of those marvellous dramatic moments which impress themselves on the memories of the audience for ever. Many other great names have trod the boards at the Theatre Royal in the course of its long history. Shortly after the re-opening of the theatre following renovation in 1897, the cast list for the London Lyceum Company's production of The Merchant of Venice featured Ellen Terry as Portia, with the great Henry Irving in the role of Shylock.

Above right: There is a very fine lamp, which we take to be a gas lamp, on the building to the left; behind it we can see the name of Harrington Street, while closer to the camera on the other side of the road is Currant Street. In the background is The Castle inn. None of these clues is likely to be of much assistance to a modern reader trying to identify the location, however. Harrington Street and Currant Street, which ran off Sussex Street, were among the network of streets swept away by slum clearance schemes in the 1930s. This area was once densely populated; however, it had poor sanitation and few amenities, and by Victorian times it was classed as a slum. In the early 20th century, the trend was for residential development to be focused around the fringes of the existing settlement, so Nottingham grew outwards and the inner city fell into decay. Between the two wars around 17,000 families from this area were rehoused, and land clearance was already in progress when this photograph was taken in 1931. By 1933 much demolition had taken place, although some properties remained standing until the late 1960s.

Right:
Bridlesmith Gate is one of Nottingham's attractive, narrow shopping streets. It is seen here from its junction with St Peter's Gate, in the days before the area was paved; the photograph was probably taken around 1955. On the left-hand side we can see the entrance to King John's Arcade, a glazed arcade, tiny by modern standards, which runs back from Bridlesmith Gate. Many of the old buildings seen here survived the 20th century without significant alteration, although bit by bit structures along this street are being replaced; at the time of writing, a demolition and reconstruction project is going on behind hoardings a short way beyond King John's Arcade. The overhanging upper storeys ('jetties') and bay windows are restrained compared with the medieval areas of some other towns, where citizens in opposite buildings can almost shake hands across the street, but still give a dignified and picturesque quality to the townscape.

Below: Long Row is seen here during World War II; we can see the sign on Jays' shop which directs people to the air raid shelter, should the wail of the sirens suddenly begin.

The black and white markings along the edge of the pavement were put there to help people negotiate the kerb during the blackout, and the white stripe along the rear of the bus served a similar purpose. Nearer the camera is Henry Farmer's music shop - not to be confused with Farmer's the drapers, famous for their store on Poultry which until 1974 occupied the former site of Smith's Bank. Next to Farmer's music shop, which in more recent years became a branch of Boots, is Pearsons' departmental store, which served the people of Nottingham for just one hundred years, having opened in 1889 and closed down in 1989. After the war alterations were made to the upper part of the frontage, with the addition of a row of gables. The firm opened a second store in Empire House, Upper Parliament Street, in the 1960s. When they ceased trading, their Upper Parliament Street premises were demolished, but the Long Row building was preserved with Grade II listed status, as the frontage was found to be concealing the timber frames of two Georgian houses. The building survived a fire which badly damaged the interior in 1996.

Below: In the foreground of the photograph we can see a heap of planks and sundry construction equipment that warn of impending works in Lister Gate. The year is 1950, so it is not yet time to begin work on the Broadmarsh Centre; in fact arrangements are being made to demolish the Walter Fountain, which has stood here since 1866 but which has now become a hazard to traffic. The fountain was erected as a memorial to John Walter MP, who was an influential local figure in the town in the 1830s and 40s, and also editor and chief proprietor of The Times. Like another 19th century local politician of a different party who was also commemorated for a time by a monument in the city - and like many politicians since - John Walter found his career heading for the rocks when his integrity was brought into question. Allegations of bribery were levelled against his supporters following his success in a by-election, sufficient evidence was found, and John Walter was disqualified from office. This happened in 1841; John Walter died in 1847, and his son, also called John Walter, erected the fountain as a memorial in 1866. Had the memorial appeared a year or so sooner, it might perhaps have served as a salutary warning to Samuel Morley, who suffered a similar disgrace in 1865.

Right: Two-way traffic was permitted along Carlton Street and Goose Gate in 1950 when this picture was taken and it was perhaps time to give some thought to making it one way. Nottingham was the first provincial city to introduce a permanent one-way system. This was in St James Street, and was implemented in 1924; one-way traffic flows had occasionally been enforced in various parts of Britain before that, but only ever on a temporary basis. This must have been quite a challenge to the motorists of the day. Indeed, newpaper reports of the new one-way system which was brought in much later as part of the 1960s urban redevelopment make amusing reading. It seems that the difficulty arose over the new 'continental' traffic signs. Before that, motorists had been warned not to enter a street by a sign which said 'No Entry'. The populace did not know quite what to make of these strange red circles with a white bar across them, so treated them with true British contempt and ignored them. Some motorists felt that the safest thing to do was to follow the police car; unfortunately the police were a little unclear about it too, and went round the system the wrong way. Finally it was all sorted out. The real problem, it transpired, had been that the signs were not in the right place, and so had been hard to see.

Both Pearson's and Griffin and Spalding's businesses, pictured here in 1949, enjoyed the custom of many generations of Nottingham shoppers. Griffin and Spalding was founded in 1846, and the Victorian building which was originally erected on this prime corner site was rebuilt and extended along Long Row in the mid-1920s. Since the acquisition of the business by Debenhams in more recent years, the store has grown larger still and now stretches a good way up Market Street. Further to the left, the superb Victorian premises of the Talbot, now Yates Wine Lodge, have been preserved and modernised. An inscription on the front of the building, high

above the entrance, informs us that the Talbot was established in 1580. In fact an inn is believed to have existed here in medieval times, but until the Tudor period it was probably known as the Bull's Head. In the early 1870s the Talbot was acquired by Edward Cox. He pulled the old building down and created in its place a truly amazing Victorian 'gin palace' where patrons could enjoy musical entertainment, and the new Talbot soon became the talk of the town. This luxurious, ornate, no-expense-spared drinkers' paradise, crammed full of intriguing objets d'art, was purchased by the Yates Wine Lodge company in 1929. It is now a Grade II listed building.

*L*ong Row East is seen here going about its business in the early years of the second world war. Prominent on the right is the Black Boy Hotel, a fine building with an interesting history, which was demolished in 1969. For centuries the site had been occupied by a hostelry. King Charles II is reputed to have stayed at the coaching inn which used to stand there; Watson Fothergill undertook its reconstruction in 1887, and the fine 19th century structure which he created was to accommodate such illustrious guests as Laurence Olivier and Gracie Fields. The Black Boy Hotel was also the first home of Nottingham Writers' Club,

which was founded at a meeting held there in 1927; some readers may recall that the Club's annual Short Story Prize was won in 1951 by a certain 21-year-old local lad, who was to go on to write a novel about Raleigh factory workers, which became a major screen hit. The novel was, of course, Saturday Night And Sunday Morning, and the author was Alan Sillitoe. However, in the end all the Black Boy's famous connections could not save it, and in spite of a great deal of local controversy Littlewoods, who purchased the site in 1963, obtained planning permission to knock the hotel down and build a modern store there.

Above: This marvellous scene was captured in Sneinton Market in 1931. There is nothing quite like the lively, friendly, uninhibited atmosphere of a bustling out-door market, and the sniff of a bargain is something that seems to retain the same attraction for every generation. The Players Please advert seen here carried no health warning, and smoking used to be regarded as perfectly socially acceptable. Our idols on the silver screen smoked, and people routinely appeared on television with cigarettes in their hands. The message that smoking can damage your health has been hammered home to us so hard in recent times that we find it difficult to imagine a time when people were not aware of it, but when medical research first identified a link between cigarettes and lung cancer, the news came as a great shock.

Top: High up on the roof, the Pearl Assurance advertisement bears the slogan 'Security and service in war and peace', alerting us to the fact that this might be a wartime scene. In fact it is; the photograph was taken in 1944, and armed with this knowledge we tend to look at shops like these, which once stood in South Parade but which no longer exist, with a new interest. How were Streamline Taxis coping with the shortage of petrol? As the war progressed some buses in Nottingham were converted to gas, and proudly travelled around with a huge gasbag on the roof. Was Bertha Knight's millinery store managing to balance its books? Items of children's clothing could be obtained without coupons, but for adults, practically every garment had its price in terms of ration points; so a new cap and gown had to be pushed firmly to the bottom of most housewives' lists, no matter how tempting the goods in Bertha Knight's window. Alfred Hind had probably done a good trade in blackout material early in the war; the amount of black fabric purchased during those first few months defies the imagination. And the Savoy Cafe was no doubt waiting impatiently for the return of good wholesome ingredients. By 1944 its staff had probably seen enough dried egg powder to last a lifetime.

This wonderful 1928 photograph of Long Row is a fascinating blend of the familiar and the unfamiliar. Long Row used to be at the heart of the city, bustling with shoppers; here it is so busy that pedestrians are spilling off the pavement into the road, though with so little traffic about, it hardly matters. Closest to the camera are Queens Chambers, the work of the gifted Victorian architect Watson Fothergill. Beyond, Dean's premises subsequently changed hands, and Van Allen had the spot for many years. H Samuel remained in the next building for a very long time. Continuing along the Row, we come to a

Lipton's, one of the chain of grocery shops established by Sir Thomas Lipton. Thomas Lipton was born in Glasgow and, so the story goes, rose from errand boy to millionaire by the age of 30; this kind of success was being replicated all over Britain around that time, with other major retail names such as Boots, Littlewoods and Marks & Spencer all being founded by one or two individuals, and going on to make a fortune. Lipton's building was taken over by the YWCA during the second world war. The white building beyond was Long Row Picture House at the time of this photograph, and was turned into a Lyons coffee house two years later.

Dominating the parade of shops to the left of Upper Parliament Street is Nottingham Co-operative Society's main store, with the giant letters NCS on the roof visible from many streets away. The Co-operative movement made a very real difference to the lives of the workers throughout the first part of the 20th century, bringing them everyday goods at prices they could afford. Local Co-operative societies were formed in most towns and cities. Rochdale, of course, is widely regarded as the place where the Co-operative movement all began, and certainly it was the Rochdale Pioneers who in the mid-19th century introduced the system of dividend payments which then became standard practice throughout the movement. Divi became one of the Co-op's great attractions, and each family's divi number was permanently etched into the memories of even its youngest member, to be quoted whenever they made any purchase, however small - it all adds up! At first each co-operative society operated independently, but from February 1949 the Co-op National Membership Scheme was launched. This meant that Co-op members qualified for divi on purchases from any co-operative society, not just their own - or, as the slogan put it, 'She shall have 'divi' wherever she goes!' In addition to its retail outlets, the Co-op offered insurance and funeral services which helped set many people's minds at rest about the future at a time when few such assurance schemes existed.

Right: The nation's shopping habits changed tremendously in the course of the 20th century. Self-service stores and super-markets seemed strange at first; taking goods from the shelf and putting them into your basket seemed almost like stealing. On the whole we felt safer shopping at the corner shop, where we could catch up on the local gossip. Shopkeepers looked after their regular customers, making sure they kept their favourite brands in stock; and if someone came knocking on the back door after the shop had closed, having just run out of some vital ingredient, then they were never turned away. But as more and more families acquired cars, the supermarket began to lure customers away from the small shops. There was more choice, there was a car park right outside, and the supermarkets could afford to cut prices in a way that a local shop never could. The parade of shops seen here in 1966 is in Radford Road, and Hyson Green is a case in point. Local residents used to rely on shops like these for their day to day needs. Then a shopping centre was built. And by the end of the 20th century, a giant supermarket had moved in.

Below: The policeman in the foreground would be standing with his back to the Broadmarsh Shopping Centre on an equivalent snapshot taken 35 years later. This photograph was taken at the corner of Bridlesmith Gate and Middle Pavement in 1937, when butchers' boys still flew around the city on their bicycles. The building on the left-hand corner of Bridlesmith Gate used to be the Sun Insurance office, and above the door we can see a giant model of the old Sun fire sign. Fire insurance companies used to attach their own fire sign to the buildings of their clients. Each insurance company had its own fire brigade, and when an alarm was sounded, fire brigades would rush out to inspect the burning premises. If the building bore the fire sign of their own company, they would set about extinguishing the blaze, but if not they would go away again and leave it for their rivals to deal with. Prudent landlords and proprietors would take out insurance with a number of societies; the building would then display an array of fire signs, which would improve its chances of receiving prompt attention. A number of old fire signs have been preserved on buildings around the city centre.

By the mid-1960s, this view of the city was no longer to the liking of the town planners and other forward-looking citizens. Urban life and social values had changed a great deal since the second world war, and the time was fast approaching when Nottingham would have to adopt a comprehensive strategy to deal with this. The traffic issue had already been addressed in the 1950s, and bold steps had been taken to slice across the city with a new road. The construction of Maid Marian Way - or rather, the destruction of some of the historic property which this entailed - had created a certain amount of ill-feeling. Now the city was planning to adapt itself to the needs of the post-war consumer society by creating indoor shopping complexes, and at the same it proposed to improve the housing situation by introducing high-rise living. It was perhaps inevitable, especially in the wake of the Maid Marian Way controversy, that proposals for further radical redevelopment should be met with opposition, and sure enough they were. People were unhappy to lose the picturesque Drury Hill in the Broad Marsh scheme, and the sacrifice of Victoria Station for the Victoria Centre was unpopular too. Neither did people want a sky-scraper in the middle of the cityscape. But change had to come, and both the Broad Marsh and Victoria centres were opened in the 1970s.

Bottom: This photograph, taken in Radford Road, Hyson Green, has the mid-1960s written all over it - even without the give-away C-registration plates of the Ford Anglia and the Mk I Cortina, hailing back to the days when registration letters changed but once a year. The upper-storey window of the building in the left foreground is tempting ladies to get into girdles, with a 30-day trial offer (it is hard not to wonder what happened if, at the end of the 30 days, you decided you didn't want it; could you take it back?). Fashion models like Twiggy were setting a trend for being thin that drove mothers of teenage girls to despair, and the prospect of looking five to six pounds thinner, without suffering too much in the process, would hold great appeal for a generation of highly figure-conscious ladies. The generation gap was yawning: those who had done too much enforced dieting during the war as a result of rationing and food shortages were scandalised to see their offspring counting calories and renouncing butter in favour of margarine, though they were even more scandalised by the length of the boys' hair and the girls' skirts. On the other side of Radford Road, Alberta's radio and TV shop reminds us of that great, new influence of the 60s - television. In 1960 there were 10.5 million television sets in Britain, and by 1968 there were 19 million.

Right: Motorists learned to keep their eyes peeled, and pedestrians grew accustomed to having to pick their way across the rubble and mud at this junction while major road construction was under way. Work on Maid Marian Way seemed to go on for ever. The first phase was more or less completed by the end of the 50s, but at that stage the road was still single

carriageway. Further demolition to the east (city-centre side) was necessary in order to convert it to dual carriageway. Finally the roundabout could be finished, the junction layout finalised and pedestrian subways built. In the meanwhile, the modern, multi-storey office block City House had arisen to further transform the area. And while all this was taking place, there were constant rumblings of discontent in background. Although it was true that rush-hour traffic jams were becoming a problem, many people still resented seeing the layout of their city hacked around in this way; but it was the loss of the city's heritage through the demolition of buildings that was felt most keenly, and bitter complaints were made about this. Perhaps most lamented of all were Abel Collin's Almshouses, a quadrangle of almshouses of great architectural merit which from 1709 to 1956 stood on the very spot seen in this photograph.

The view looking northwards along High Street towards Clumber Street changed significantly in the second half of the 1950s. Up to the middle of the decade, Skinner and Rook's high-class grocery establishment continued to occupy the prominent position on the corner of Long Row where High Street narrows into Clumber Street. There was always a wonderful aroma inside the shop; Skinner and Rook was one of the old-fashioned type of provisions merchants, selling fruit and vegetables, fine wines, cheeses and freshly-roasted coffee. However, in 1955 this shop closed and the site was sold for redevelopment. This photograph, taken in 1958, shows the new retail and office block that went up in its place.

This was one of Nottingham's first experiments with the modern look, and during the 1960s many more structures were to be built in this style - square, plain and practical, with sharp, straight, clear lines, a lot of windows and minimal ornamentation. Since this picture was taken the area shown here has changed in character as well as in appearance as a result of the opening of the two shopping centres. The Kardomah cafe, which used to stand opposite Skinner and Rook, has now disappeared. The Boots name has also vanished from the High Street; the big Boots seen here on the right closed in 1972 when the business was transferred to the Victoria Shopping Centre, and the fine premises seem a little unsure of their next role at the time of writing.

The People's War

Above: We believe that these youngsters may be Southend schoolchildren. However, documentary records of identities and locations were deliberately blurred during the war, in order to prevent the enemy obtaining any precise information which might be useful. Even when air raids were reported in the newspaper, places were never referred to by name, but in terms as vague as 'a city in the South' or 'a town in the Midlands'. So officially we are looking at a photograph of evacuees 'from South East coastal areas' (although it has also been suggested that they are Nottingham schoolchildren) arriving in a village generally agreed to be 'somewhere in Nottinghamshire.' Each child would have had a label firmly attached to their person, and was allowed to bring one medium-sized bag, which would contain their gas mask, sandwiches, a change of clothes - and their favourite toy. Their parents also gave them a self-addressed envelope, which would be posted back when the child was settled, giving the address of the host family. Sometimes children were not told what was happening, and embarked on the train thinking that they were going for a day trip, and would be returning home in the evening. However, the rather set expressions on some of the little faces suggest that they know something out of the ordinary is happening, even if they are not as yet quite sure what it is.

Winston Churchill declared the nation to be at war with Germany on 3rd September, 1939, and later that same month the Emergency Committee began organising its schedule of evacuations. All over Britain the priority was to get children away from areas which were likely to be targeted by the enemy bombers. Families who were able to do so made their own arrangements; many went to stay with relatives who lived away from the high-risk areas. In the majority of cases this made for very cramped living conditions, and no bombs seemed to be landing, so after spending a few months in the country an increasing number of families began to drift back home again. The following year, however, air raids began in earnest, and a second major evacuation exercise took place. For those families who were not able to stay together, it was an emotional time. Having seen their husbands march off to the front, mothers had to worry about packing their children off to stay with complete strangers, and not knowing when they would see them again. The most important thing was that their offspring were safe. However, some host families had the unenviable task of breaking the sad news to very small evacuees that their families had been killed in a bombing raid. The families who were able to stay together were the lucky ones.

*T*he waiting vehicles and the crowds standing around with luggage might almost have been setting off on a pleasure trip, were it not for the arm-bands which identify them as evacuees. Evacuations during WW2 were organised by a special Emergency Committee. Sometimes evacuees were simply moved out of their homes in the city to the nearby countryside, which we think was the case in this photograph, but sometimes they had to travel much further. In all, around 5,000 were evacuated from Nottingham itself, and though most went to towns and villages in Nottinghamshire, some were sent to other counties. Children from London and the densely-populated areas in the South East could expect to be scattered all over the country; some cities even sent their children abroad. As can be imagined, all this led to a glorious mix of accents, social backgrounds and lifestyles in the parts of Britain which were receiving evacuees; children who had grown up in the Nottinghamshire countryside got to know children from inner cities who had never seen a cow before. For most people involved in the evacuation programme, the experience was on the whole positive, though some unfortunately had a miserable and traumatic time of it - and probably nobody enjoyed the first few moments at their new home, when to add to the emotional uncertainty, the new arrivals had to be subjected to a thorough inspection for nits, lice and other such uninvited guests.

The declaration of war was not a time to sit around worrying about what might happen - there was work to be done! All over Britain, citizens threw themselves into preparations for the defence of their towns and cities. Some discovered talents they didn't know they had; certainly some men and women discovered the delights and blisters of manual labour for the first time in their lives. This bustling scene from 1939 shows the staff of City Hospital and Vale Brook Lodge organising themselves into filling sandbags. Civic buildings all over the country relied on piles of sandbags to protect them from bomb damage - although in the case of a direct hit, no amount of sandbags could prevent the inevitable from happening. Another protective measure commonly seen in town centres was shop windows criss-crossed with tape; the purpose of this was to prevent occupants and passers-by being injured by pieces of flying glass, if the window shattered. The painting of white markings at strategic points on the pavement and street furniture was another essential task which had to be carried out in preparation for the blackout. Travelling was hazardous when it was pitch dark, and pedestrians and motorists would have had little chance of avoiding lamp-posts, kerbs and suchlike, had these obstacles not been picked out with white stripes.

Below: Compared to cities such as Coventry, Nottingham suffered relatively little damage during the second world war. This, however, would have been scant consolation to those who lost their homes or their loved ones during the night of 8th-9th May, 1941. Statistics of that night's blitz on Nottingham make grim reading. A total of 424 high explosive bombs landed on the city. Damage was caused to more than 4,500 homes, of which around 450 were so badly wrecked that they were no longer fit to live in afterwards. This photograph shows the disastrous aftermath at the site of the University College, part of which has collapsed; other public buildings which suffered included the Moot Hall, the Registrar's and Poor Law offices, the churches of St John and St Christopher, the Boots printing works on Station Street, the new office block in Castle Gate, and a number of shops - amongst them Armitage's store on the corner of Victoria Street and High Street, and shops near the Moot Hall at the corner of Friar Lane. At the LMS railway station almost a hundred passenger coaches were destroyed or damaged. The Co-op bakery in Meadow Lane was flattened, and sadly it was here that heavy casualties were recorded; of the 49 fatalities and 20 injuries which occurred at this spot, the vast majority were Co-op employees.

Bottom: A Moot Hall was the name given to early town halls, used for various civic and public purposes, and sometimes as courts. Nottingham's used to stand in Friar Lane. This scene of wreckage shows what was left of the Moot Hall and its neighbour H Wilkinson & Co after the night of 8th-9th May, 1941. The mock-Georgian Moot Hall which has just been reduced to rubble was built around 1900. It replaced an earlier Moot Hall, a 17th century building which had formerly served as one of Nottingham's old inns, known as The Feathers. By contrast, the hall which took its place was to serve the city for barely four decades before being wiped out by enemy action. But the citizens of Nottingham had more to worry about than the loss of their Moot Hall. During the night the emergency services had been called out to around a hundred fires; six rest centres were very busy coping with the 1,286 people who had been bombed out; and there were casualties to be taken care of. Doubtless the horror of the raid left Nottingham shocked and saddened, and perhaps trying to draw some small comfort from the knowledge that but for the 'starfish site' at Cropwell Butler, the consequences might have been even worse; fires lit here as a decoy had succeeded in fooling almost a hundred enemy bombers, who dropped their bombs on the open countryside instead of Nottingham.

Bottom: Mobile canteens, or tea cars, were not merely a handy place to get a little extra snack during the war; they were a necessity. Apart from the NAAFI (the organisation responsible for catering for HM Forces), a number of civilian organisations including the WVS and the YMCA operated tea cars, which were for the most part staffed by volunteers. Wherever people were engaged on civil defence and rescue work, at whatever time of the day or night, and whatever the circumstances might be - regular duties, a special training exercise or a real emergency - the appearance of a mobile canteen meant that at least there was the prospect of a hot drink and something to eat, to keep up the strength and the spirits of troops and civilian workers alike. However, on the occasion pictured here the tea car has not come along to serve a tired and thirsty crowd - the crowd has come along to see the new tea car. Tea car number 234 was a generous gift from Messrs Bairns-Wear, and this photograph was taken on the occasion of its presentation by the company and acceptance on behalf of the YMCA by the Duke of Portland, on 7th May, 1940.

Right: War is an expensive business. During WW2, Nottingham certainly did its bit to put money into the coffers to provide Britain's armed forces with the equipment they needed. Each year, a week was set aside for parades and publicity to focus attention on the particular objective for which funds were being raised that year; after all, there's nothing like the pomp and glory of a full-scale, impeccably-choreographed military parade to get people

dipping into their pockets. So in 1940 we had War Weapons Week; in 1942 we had the Tanks for Attack campaign; 1943 featured Wings for Victory Week; and 1944's Salute the Soldier week raised the largest sum of all - £4,044,420. Our photograph shows the fund-raising parade during 1942, and the float clearly tells us what the theme is this time: yes, it's Warship Week! Dominating the scene is a huge poster fixed to the front of Council House which tells us that we must save £10,000,000 during 1941 for the 20 destroyers; Warship Week succeeded in raising £2,817,646 towards this. The message on the banners behind the line of troops standing smartly to attention to the right of our picture is partially obscured. We can read 'Ships and Guns - They'll Blast . .' but the end of the message is not visible. 'The Huns', perhaps?

Above: Women were an essential labour force during the second world war. They took over a multitude of roles that in peace time had been the male preserve, from becoming bakers to joining the Land Army and working on the farms. Many women went into uniform, sometimes military and sometimes not. In civilian life they donned the uniforms of postal workers, bus drivers and conductors - even chauffeuses; officials from Nottingham Corporation had the privilege of being driven around by some very smart lady chauffeuses during WW2. The girls seen in this photograph, however, have taken the military option and joined the Auxiliary Territorial Service, the women's section of the army. They were called upon to perform a wide variety of duties, including working on tanks which were to be sent overseas. Chilwell Central Ordnance Depot was responsible for providing tanks and other army transport, and around 5,000 men and women were employed there, round the clock. Many ATS personnel had to undergo special training to prepare them for their new duties, and were expected to rapidly pick up the basic principles of engineering and master the necessary skills. Strict military discipline and drilling was also required of them. Here, the girls are seen marching off the parade ground after an inspection.

Top: Say 'wartime parades' and the words conjure up the tramp of heavy boots, the gleam of polished buttons, and perhaps even the glint of weapons; but this is a parade of a slightly different nature. The occasion pictured here is the Joint Church Parade of the Red Cross and St John Ambulance Brigade at St Mary's Church, during 1940. These two organisations gave admirable service during the second world war. Not only were they constantly exposed to the trauma of dealing with casualties who had suffered terrible injuries, but they were also called upon to attend disasters where they sometimes had to be prepared to risk their own lives in order to search for survivors or fatalities in the wreckage after an explosion, when fire or the presence of gas made the situation hazardous. Nottingham had twelve First Aid Posts and three mobile first aid units; the rule of thumb was that there should be one FAP to every 15,000 people. FAPs were manned by a doctor, a trained nurse and nursing auxiliaries. First Aid Parties were composed of four men and a driver, all experienced first-aid workers trained by the Red Cross, the St John Ambulance or St Andrew's Society. Thanks to their bravery and their devotion, over and above the call of duty, suffering and loss of life was minimised. We take great pleasure in including this photograph in our collection.

Above: Civil Defence workers had to be prepared to meet every conceivable kind of emergency situation which might result from enemy action during World War Two: rescuing people from bombed buildings, decontaminating the area after a gas attack (which, of course, never came), and - as shown here - dealing with passengers on a train who have been injured by machine-gun fire. Happily, the absence of bullet-holes in the carriages reassures us that in fact this was a practice, and not a real incident. Our gallant army of defence workers nobly gave up their spare time to take part in training exercises such as this - along with all the extras who played the part of the victims, as rather than use dummies for war exercises of this nature, local people were recruited. Indeed, the scenes were made so realistic that it is sometimes difficult to be sure whether a photograph shows a practice or an actual rescue operation. In this case it was definitely the former; this was Nottingham's big ARP practice, which took place early in the war. Although thankfully no machine gun attack ever transpired, the ARP's first aid skills and stretchering expertise were put to the test on a number of occasions, notably during the bombing raid of the night of 8th May, 1941. Co-incidentally, a great deal of damage was inflicted to passenger trains at the LMS station - but fortunately they were empty at the time.

Above right: This very male gathering - of whom only the vicar appears to have heeded the oft-repeated public advice to always carry his gas mask - is watching Mr G B H Wilson, the local Chairman of the National War Savings Committee in Nottingham, start the model racing car on its journey up the Midlands Barometer for War Savings. The year is 1940, and who knows how long the war will last; all anybody can do is hope and pray that the little car's journey will be rapid, but above all brief. All over Britain, people were urged to contribute as much to the defence budget as they could afford, principally through investing in National Savings Certificates. Three per cent Defence Bonds could be bought at banks or post offices in units of £5, or by instalments by purchasing 2/6d National Savings Stamps. These Bonds were repayable after seven years, with a bonus of one shilling per £5 invested. Other options included two per cent National War Bonds and three per cent Savings Bonds. Each town and city kept a running total of the amount invested in these schemes by its citizens, and this became a matter of great civic pride. In recognition, Spitfires and other fighting machines would be named after the towns and cities whose money had financed their construction. Twenty-five Churchill tanks were named 'City of Nottingham'.

The year is 1949, and the Embankment steps are packed with spectators who have gathered to enjoy the sunshine and watch the Quincentenary River Carnival. Spectacles included an impressive fire-launch display by the City Fire Brigade, who demonstrated their ability to extinguish a blazing vessel with powerful jets of water. The Quincentenary was designed to provide entertainment for all the family, and we can see that the River Carnival has attracted all age groups. Nottingham was celebrating the anniversary of the Royal Charter which recognised its growing importance by creating the county of Nottingham, and 500 years on the city was continuing to grow. Council housing estates were being created, particularly around Bulwell and Bilborough; work on the largest of the new residential estates, at Clifton, would commence in a couple of years, following an extension of the city boundary in 1951. Then as now, Nottingham was a good place to live. It had pleasant parks and gardens, sporting activities, and plenty of entertainment in the form of dance halls, an Ice Stadium and a large number of cinemas. There were good shops and a market. Work was available both for women and for men, with Boots, Raleigh and Players being the three major employers. A secure job, a comfortable home, and good leisure facilities - what more could you ask of a city?

High days & holidays

Above: Primary school sports are in progress on the Forest in this photograph, and these activities were part of the 1949 Quincentenary celebrations. The city's schoolchildren were well represented in the programme of events. Two junior schools, Trent Bridge and Henry Whipple, joined forces in presenting the Pageant of Robin Hood and King John at the Albert Hall. Henry Whipple Junior School, on the Bestwood estate, was named after the city's first Director of Education, who in 1924 had planned the construction of a number of schools to serve the communities on the new council estates. However, work on the Bestwood estate had been interrupted by war, and the school was new in 1949. Every effort had been made to keep school life as normal as possible during the war, but a certain amount of disruption had been inevitable - not least because of all the evacuations which were taking place. One school in the area, for instance, shared its premises with a school from Southend which had been evacuated to the Midlands, with the Nottingham pupils having lessons in the morning and the Essex pupils in the afternoon.

Above right: Show a small boy a tank, and he won't be able to resist clambering all over it! Even the girls have deigned to take an interest in this particular tank, which was on display at Wollaton Park at the time of the 1953 coronation. The idea of a tank - alias an armoured personnel carrier - is so wonderfully simple and yet so complex, with all those fascinating sticking-out bits that swivel and tilt - and is that the button you press to make it shoot? The British Army pinned great hopes to its new secret weapon, the tank, in the first world war. Shipped to France in crates marked 'water tanks' - a clever and devious ploy to fool the enemy - these armoured vehicles were first used on 15th December 1916 at the Battle of the Somme. Their tracks meant that they could travel over rough terrain that wheeled vehicles could never have crossed; but they were not as reliable as had been hoped, and fuel shortages and mechanical breakdowns limited their effectiveness. In the second world war, tanks were used again, but engineers were instructed to turn their attention to designing airborne fighting machines . . . and the rest is history.

To a 21st century reader, the word 'tram' almost invariably conjures up the image of an electric tram clickety-clacking along tramlines, complete with all its overhead paraphernalia. The first trolley buses were sometimes referred to, rather paradoxically, as 'trackless trams' because, like trams, they had overhead cables and trolley poles. Some modern dictionaries even define a tram as an electrically-powered vehicle. In fact, of course, the first trams were horse-drawn. Trams are simply vehicles which run along tracks, as opposed to buses, which don't. Having sorted out the difference between the two, all is then thrown into confusion again by the legend on the side of this fine vehicle, photographed during Nottingham's Transport Jubilee in 1947; here we have a horse-drawn bus, clearly labelled Nottingham Corporation Tramways. Tram or bus, its function is clear, and many people have seized the opportunity to clamber up and enjoy a ride on the open top deck. Private operators began to develop a horse tramway network in Nottingham in the last decades of the 19th century; the first horse tram went between the Market Place and Basford in 1881, and the stables were on Isandula Road. The tramway system was acquired by the Corporation in 1897, hence its 50 year jubilee in 1947.

A century of growing and growth

In a world where things come and go with increasing speed and regularity the story of T. Hammond & Sons, celebrating its centenary in 2000, is one to give heart to the gloomiest sceptic.

The business was founded in 1900 by Thomas Hammond, the eldest son of a frame-work knitter who lived with his wife and seven children in a cottage at the top of Church Lane, Arnold. Life for the Hammond family was as frugal as it was for any worker's at the time; spring water, earth closets, paraffin lamps and candles.

Aged ten, with little work available locally, he was sent to London to live and work for his uncle, an innkeeper and butcher in the rough dockland area of Rotherhythe. An unhappy, lonely four years followed during which time he did not return home. At times, when feeling very homesick he would go to St. Pancras Station and watch the trains departing for Nottingham, a little dog was his only friendly company. The fighting, the prostitution and drunken behaviour of the dockland area affected him profoundly. In later years he was reluctant to enter public houses or discuss this period of his life.

Aged 14 he returned home and found work with Thomas Dabell, a market gardener at Derry Mount, Arnold. His starting wage with Mr. Dabell was 2/6d. per week rising to 18/-d. per week when a man. Mr. Dabell had a son and three daughters and he hoped that on his retirement the business would pass to his son.

Above centre: Thomas and Annie Hammond, with sons Tom and Jack c.1910. Below: A watercolour of Derry Mount Yard c.1930.

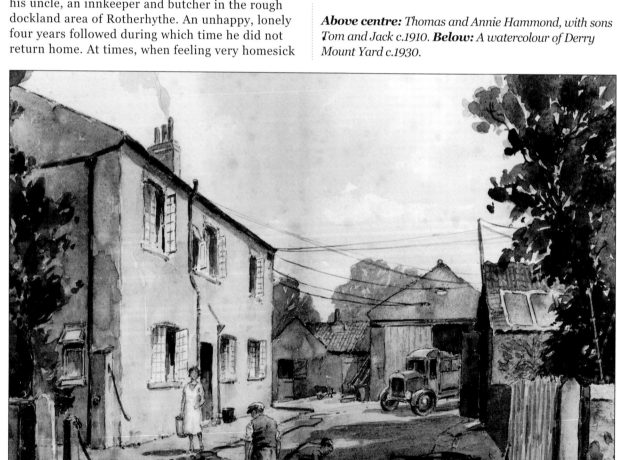

However, after a period the son found he had no wish to follow his father, he left Derry Mount and later became a Doctor.

In the late 1890s, Mr. Dabell was considering retirement. Thomas Hammond, who by this time was a capable Market Gardener and a senior member of staff, saw his opportunity and asked him if there was any way he might take over the business. Naturally, Mr. Dabell asked whether Thomas had any money, in fact he had saved over 100 sovereigns during his employment. Mr. Dabell's response was that if Thomas had saved that much whilst working for him, he was perfectly capable and suitable to take on the business. Arrangements were made, Thomas paid the deposit with interest to be paid on the balance, the capital was to be repaid as and when he could. It was a measure of the older man's regard for Thomas that this transaction was concluded without any involvement of the legal profession, Mr. Dabell also gave a reference of his character and standing to the bank. Another reference was supplied by the Reverend Truman of St. Mary's Church, Arnold where Thomas had been a chorister since his return from London.

On March 25th 1900 at the age of 28 years, Thomas Hammond became proprietor of his own business and in the same year he married Annie Herring, the eldest daughter of a local builder. They moved into Derry Mount, the Hammond family's occupation of which was to last nearly 70 years. He bought the business but not the land and buildings of the 12 acre holding, the land was rented from two spinster ladies, the Misses Charles of Bulwell, Nottingham. The produce from this holding was sold on the Nottingham Wholesale Market where Thomas had assisted Mr Dabell in his later years. The tenancy of the stand was transferred along with the business in 1900.

Produce was transported to market on horse drawn drays that weighed up to a ton. When heavier loads were required an extra gear horse was taken to give assistance on the Sherwood and Gallows Hill inclines. In icy weather the horses were 'studded up' to prevent them slipping on the frozen cobbles. The trip of four and half miles would take up to an hour and a half and with the early opening times of the market, they had to rise at a very early hour to prepare the horses and set off. At this time all local deliveries of produce from the wholesale market were by horse and dray. The railway was used for deliveries to more distant towns such as Mansfield and Sutton-in-Ashfield. Fruit vans were attached to the rear of the early morning local passenger trains for this purpose. The Fruit Merchants and Greengrocers from the outlying towns would often accompany their produce and ride in the vans to ensure its security and safe arrival.

The drays, after any necessary deliveries would not return direct to Derry Mount. They would call at large local stables, particularly Shipstones the brewers and collect horse manure. This was brought back to the market garden and spread on the land. True efficiency, the drays would be loaded both ways and seldom made empty journeys. This would however add hours to what was already a very long day. The practise of collecting horse manure for the farm continued with motor transport until the 1950s.

Annie Hammond proved to be an astute business-woman. She assisted Thomas at market in the early years by acting as his clerk and looking after the money. When the tramcars were extended to Arnold she travelled to market on the 6.00am tram. At the close of business they would both return to Arnold by tram.

Above: *Thomas Hammond's bill of sale for the Derry Mount business - March 1900.*

Annie also dealt with the wages and all other 'office affairs' in the kitchen at Derry Mount.

Thomas and Annie had four children; Tom, Jack, Dorothy and the eldest, Maggie, who alas died in infancy. Whilst Thomas and Annie were putting in very long hours building the business, the children were looked after by Annie's unmarried sister, Eliza, who lived with them at Derry Mount. She was much loved by the children and her contribution to family life and the business was enormous.

Derry Mount was a rented holding and Thomas developed his business by renting small parcels of adjacent land, which at that time provided no long term security of tenure. In 1924 he purchased 20 acres of nearby land to develop the business and secure the future. The timing of this purchase was unfortunate in that it was followed immediately by the decision of the Misses Charles to sell the Derry Mount holding. The holding was sold to a wealthy local estate owner for the mineral rights. He had no other interest and promptly offered it for resale. Thomas found himself with no option but to make a second major purchase or lose Derry Mount.

A family anecdote goes that Thomas had to visit the estate owner to finalise the sale. The deal was struck and the estate owner instructed his butler to 'take Hammond to the kitchen and give him a beer and some cheese'. An insight into the view that some of the gentry had of the working class as recently as the 1920s.

Above: *Albert Colledge (centre) with other members of staff - Nottingham Wholesale Market in 1938.*
Below: *Thomas Hammond and son, Jack - Nottingham Wholesale Market 1938.*

Within two years of taking on the crippling financial burden of the two sites, the country was sliding into the major recession of the late twenties and later the depression of the thirties. A very difficult time for the recently expanded business.

Tom Hammond (jnr) left school in 1922 and soon after was made a partner. Jack left school three years later and the firm became T. Hammond & Sons. The firm had survived and recovered from the financial difficulties of the late twenties and early thirties when Thomas 'retired' in 1937. He told his sons that things should carry on as normal and Jack was to collect him at the usual early hour for the following mornings market - so retirement in name only.

On retirement, Thomas and Annie moved to a nearby property, 'Orchard Close'. At this time, Jack Hammond married Norah Walker and they moved into the family home at Derry Mount. After their marriage, Norah assisted in the farm office, an involvement that would last for the next 25 years.

In 1934, Tom Hammond (jnr) married Mary, the daughter of Harry Lamin, a well-to-do tenant farmer on the Bestwood Estate. Her family home was Top House Farm, a prize winning holding

which, at the 1915 Royal Show held in Nottingham won the 'Best Holding in Three Counties for Medium Sized Farms' taking the prize of £100; a small fortune at that time. Incidentally, the Hammonds now work much of the land that comprised Top House Farm.

Although Mary's upbringing was farming and all her ambitions were in that direction, her mother didn't consider it a suitable occupation for a young lady and so Mary was found employment as a Milliner in a high quality ladies dress shop in Nottingham. After her marriage she quickly and willingly adapted to life on a market garden whether in office, field or packing shed at any time day or night. Now in her 91st year she still takes a most active interest in all matters.

Throughout the very difficult years of the late 1920s and early 30s bankruptcy was a daily threat to most farmers and growers.

The survival of T Hammond & Sons was lead by the small dedicated team of Thomas, his sons Tom and Jack, the foreman Sam Foster and his successor, Albert Colledge.

Top: *Thomas and Annie Hammond (seated) with their family, Jack, Dorothy and Tom.*

Sam Foster started work with Thomas in 1902 on leaving school at the age of 12. A capable craftsman with both hand and horse who led by example, a hard taskmaster with very high standards, he would not suffer fools gladly.

Albert Colledge started work aged 12 years and four months in 1917. Apart from a few months at 19 years of age when he worked at Gedling Pit, Albert worked for T Hammond & Sons for 72 years. Albert succeeded Sam Foster as foreman in the late 1930s and became indispensable to the business. An honest, blunt, direct and when required demanding man his skills and experience as a market gardener and manager of staff were unrivalled. He was also highly competent at both selling and dealing with produce in the wholesale market. He 'retired' from the farming side in 1972 but still stood market for another 17 years until his 84th birthday and, by virtue of his positive attitude and integrity, was much respected throughout the growing and market community.

Albert's contribution was immense, and should the firm go on to celebrate 200 years, his like will not be seen again.

Thomas Hammond continued to attend market throughout the war years. He also continued with lighter duties about the farm - typically bunching thyme and sage in the herb room at Derry Mount often known as the 'Fire Watching Shed'. He died in 1946 leaving behind him a business founded on honesty, hard work and care for the land.

The firm first invested in motor transport in 1925, a Model T Ford. From then, this improved transport was used to purchase additional

Top: Steam cultivation at New Farm in Autumn 1949. Tom Hammond driving a John Fowler ploughing engine built in 1874. **Above centre:** *Hammonds' stand in the Wholesale Market, 7.30am, 9th February 1989. Albert Colledge with customers celebrating his forthcoming retirement.*

produce from other farms and increase the volume of product sold through the stand at the wholesale market. In the late 1930s irrigation was installed to ensure quality and continuity of crops; a pioneering and far-sighted development for that time.

New Farm was, in 1863, aptly named as the last farm to be built on the Bestwood Estate; family seat of the Duke of St Albans, the illegitimate son of Nell Gwyn and King Charles II. The farm, comprising some 200 acres was purchased in 1940 when the estate was sold off and is the present day base for T Hammond & Sons. Unfortunately, it was in a run down and dilapidated state and some £3,000 was required to bring the buildings up to standard. Within a short time and due to the demands of the second world war, over 400 pigs were housed in the farm buildings. Also at that time a steam ploughing set was acquired to assist with the additional acreage and the improvements

required to bring New Farm from traditional grassland up to vegetable growing capability. The 'Womens Land Army' was formed for the war years to fill the manpower gap left by conscription of all able young men into the forces. Hammond's used a team of 'Land Girls' doing all manner of work to help maximise food production in Britain during this time of austerity.

Further adjacent land was added in 1949 when 'Stockings Farm' became available. This adjoined the original holding at Derry Mount and made a total land base of 330 acres.

This again was a very dilapidated grassland farm and required considerable effort and capital to improve both the buildings and land.

After the war years, with the additional acreage of Stockings Farm and less pressure on food

production, Tom and Jack put part of New Farm into grass leys. They stocked heavily with cattle both to rest the fields from vegetable cropping and build up fertility without the use of manure, the availability of which had become less due to the rapid decline in the use of horses. A calf-rearing unit in the modified buildings at Stockings Farm was set up

This page: *The comparison between New Farm at purchase in 1940 (left), and New Farm 2000.*

Denis King

Denis King

under Jack's newly acquired expertise in stock-manship. The reared cattle would then graze the leys during the summer and be housed in the yards at New Farm during the winter.

The traditional market garden top and soft fruit enterprises were axed after the war years. However the production of a wide range of salad and vegetable crops continued, but on a field scale, with Tom responsible for the growing and Jack managing the marketing until the early 1960s.

From the mid 1950s, the third generation was leaving school. Tom's sons; Bill (1956), David (1959) and Michael (1962) and Jack's sons; Robert (1956) and Peter (1961).

Diverging interest now became apparent and in 1962 Tom and Jack dissolved their partnership. Derry Mount was now the base for Jack and his sons, their trading name becoming John Hammond & Co. They changed strategy to produce farm crops specialising in potatoes, sugar beet and cereals. In 1968 Jack and his family purchased a significant holding away from the area and in 1969 left Derry Mount and there, the Hammond family connection with Derry Mount ended.

New Farm became the base for Tom and his sons Bill and David who became his partners at that time. By agreement with Jack they retained the trading name of T Hammond & Sons and continued to grow a wide range of vegetable and salad crops.

Tom's youngest son, Michael, joined the business in 1963 after graduating from formal engineering training completing the partnership of Tom and three sons.

In 1969 Bill married Sheila Copley, a farmer's daughter from Upper Broughton, and moved into New Farm House. Sheila has been closely involved with the farm office from that time. David married Jane Hayes in 1988 when she, and her daughter Natalie, moved to New Farm.

In 1970, with the threat of development at New Farm and due to the requirement for good light land, a further holding at Besthorpe near Newark was acquired - west facing, very early and with irrigation it was ideally suited for all vegetable crops.

By purchase and rental this holding was quickly expanded to 250 acres and proved a very successful venture becoming Tom's special interest until his death in 1977.

A further purchase was completed in 1980 when the majority of the land became available at the adjacent Top House Farm, the childhood home of Mary Hammond (nee Lamin). Full irrigation capability was installed to bring the light, sand land into vegetable production.

Above: *A part view of the carrot packing facilities.*

brassicas and alliums on mobile rigs, were the key to the success of the business. Later, in 1994, the stand in the wholesale market was closed.

The expertise supplied by the fourth generation family members provides the cutting edge of Hammonds progress into the new Millennium. Jonathan, Bill's elder son, joined in 1992 after studying for HND in horticulture and crop production at Writtle Agricultural College, Essex. In 1995 his brother, Andrew, joined straight from Harper Adams Agricultural College, Shropshire after studying HND in Agriculture.

Today, with Bill and David, these two young men, Great Grandsons of Thomas Hammond look to the future - Jonathan managing crop technology and liasing with the major supermarket and processing customers and Andrew dealing with plant, machinery and field management.

Michael decided to follow his own path in mechanical engineering and farming taking his share of the land. His departure in 1986, coupled with the effects of the rise of supermarkets as the dominant retail force made the late 80s a very difficult trading period. The traditional high street greengrocer and the wholesale market system were in decline. It was apparent that major change was required.

With typical resilience, the Hammonds saw this as an opportunity; reduced the number of crops grown and rationalised their product lines to move forward, and indeed expand, now supplying national and regional supermarket chains and marketing their produce to major catering and processing outlets.

In order to face this period of change three distinct areas were addressed. The acquisition of more land through rental, massive investment in major washing and packing facilities and field packing of

The Firm, today in its 100th year, farms in excess of 1200 acres and employs 100 full time, part time and agency staff.

Above (both pictures): Loading produce for outward deliveries to the UK and Europe. Right: Clockwise from top left: Andrew, Jonathan , David, and Bill Hammond.

Denis King

Memorable moments

Queen Elizabeth was held in great affection by the nation from the moment her marriage to Albert, Duke of York - later King George VI - brought her into the public eye; and when her daughter came to the throne, her popularity as the Queen Mum remained as high as ever. Her beaming smile quickly earned her the nickname of The Smiling Duchess, and her taste in hats became legendary. The hat seen on this photograph is a particularly fine example. When he married Lady Elizabeth Bowes-Lyon in 1923, Prince Albert, Duke of York, was planning to pursue a career in the Navy. His elder brother Prince Edward was next in line to the throne. However, the news of Edward's involvement with the American, Mrs Wallis Simpson, hit the headlines just after the death of George V. Edward abdicated, and Albert was crowned George VI. During the war King George and Queen Elizabeth toured the country, often going to places which had suffered particularly heavy damage, and saying words of comfort to those affected. They came to Nottingham in March 1943, and stayed in the city for six hours. We are unwilling to commit ourselves as to the exact occasion of the visit pictured here, though readers may perhaps be able to confirm the details. Clearly it is not a wartime visit. It may have taken place during 1951, the year of the Festival of Britain, and the year before George VI's death.

Above: There is a fine party atmosphere in this picture. Clearly the organisers went to a lot of trouble to make Lenton Street, Hyson Green, a suitably festive setting for the children's Coronation party in 1953. They seem to have thought of everything: Union Jacks and bunting across the street, Court Jester hats for the little ones, a striped table cloth - even a special Coronation apron bearing a royal crown and the inscription Elizabeth R. The secret, of course, was to get organised in good time. Those who left it until the last minute to buy their coronation decorations were in for a disappointment, as many shops sold out of the most popular lines well before the day. Red, white and blue strip pennants cost 13s 6d for six yards, while a large rayon bunting Union Jack on a nine foot staff was priced at 19s 6d. In the city centre, traders had put up decorations to complement those provided by the council, and thousands of visitors flocked to see the splendid sight. This was good for business, so not surprisingly the shops were reluctant to take their decorations down again. The council took the view that the Queen had gone straight back to work, so they should do the same, and the council decorations came down; but many shop owners - being great cricket fans - decided to leave their decorations up until the end of the Test Match.

Right: Springfield Street, Basford, has been fortunate in choosing a bright, sunny day for their pre-Coronation party. The excited youngsters look very jolly in their assorted festive headgear; if all those red, white and blue OXO hats were obtained by saving coupons from Oxo packets, then the residents of Springfield Street must have been having gravy with everything in recent weeks, but party fare means sandwiches, jellies, trifles and cakes - all the goodies that children love. All over Nottingham, groups of neighbours had been clubbing together for weeks to organise a party for the children in their street. Everybody chipped in; as often as not, households put a shilling a week into a central kitty to go towards food, decorations, souvenirs and perhaps entertainment such as a puppet show or a ventriloquist. After the meal, each child would receive a Coronation gift - perhaps a mug, a spoon or a handkerchief. How many of these have been kept as mementoes, we wonder? Then there would be party games until bedtime, making it a day to remember for the little ones. The grown-ups, of course, would be quite exhausted by the end of the afternoon, but the sight of those happy little faces made it all worthwhile.

The Union Jacks are what this moment was all about. All that was needed to make the photograph perfect was a gust of wind, to send the big flag fluttering proudly above the heads of the patriotic crowd gathered in the Old Market Square on VE Day, 8th May, 1945. The previous day had brought the news everybody in Britain was waiting for - that Germany had surrendered unconditionally. Thousands of people in Nottingham turned out on the afternoon VE Day to listen to Winston Churchill's speech to the nation, broadcast over loudspeakers rigged up in the square. Although the war did not officially end until Japan surrendered on 14th August, VE Day marked the beginning of victory celebrations. Flags and bunting were put up in the streets and inside many business premises, and the general mood was one of elation as we looked forward to enjoying our hard-won peace after more than five and a half years of hostilities. In reality, the after-effects of the war continued to be felt for longer than many people expected. With a huge debt to pay off, rebuilding the national economy became Britain's top priority. Petrol for private use became even more scarce; sweets did not come off ration until 1949; and it was not until July 1954 that all rationing finally ended and we were able to burn those depressing ration books.

Above: Here we see the old Central Market in all its splendour, packed with shoppers and decked out for the coronation of Elizabeth II in 1953. Older readers will have fond memories of Nottingham's Central Market in King Edward Street. Opened in 1928, it enjoyed tremendous popularity with successive generations of shoppers, and in the early 1970s many people were extremely displeased to learn that it was to move to the Victoria Shopping Centre. This photograph has successfully captured the lively, bustling atmosphere of the old market hall, which was demolished in 1985. The 'Vouchers exchanged here' sign to the left reminds us that even in coronation year some items were still on ration, but by this time the depressing days of standing in queues, and trying to transform insipid ingredients into tasty, nourishing meals, were over. Things as basic as fresh eggs and butter had disappeared completely during the war, but at last they were back in the shops, white bread had lost that funny greyish tinge, and the nation was re-discovering the pleasures of shopping after years of austerity. Optimism and goodwill prevailed, and, what was more, we were genuinely thrilled to welcome to the throne our young and pretty new Queen, who had already won the affection and respect of the nation. Everybody felt that a new era was beginning in Britain, and up went the flags and banners, to show how proud we were to be British.

Below centre: Nottingham's prosperity and importance as a town grew steadily throughout medieval times, and in 1449 Henry VI granted a Charter which gave Nottingham self-governing powers and elevated it to county borough status. This was a very significant event, as without it the town would almost certainly not have developed as it has to justify the title of Queen of the Midlands. A second notable Charter was of course the one which conferred city status upon the former town of Nottingham; but without the Charter of 1449, it is entirely possible that the City Charter, granted at the time of Queen Victoria's Diamond Jubilee in 1897, would never have existed. So when this giant, illuminated horse-shoe sign appeared at Trent Bridge at the beginning of June, 1949, anybody who had so far failed to realise that it was exactly 500 years since the granting of the original Royal Charter which upgraded Nottingham's status, could remain in ignorance no longer. But most people were very well aware of the anniversary, and many had been involved in the planning of events to mark the occasion for a long time - a historical pageant, a medieval fair, a country dancing display, a river carnival, a local government exhibition and much more; and the success of the city's Quincentenary celebrations was assured when Princess Elizabeth and the Duke of Edinburgh agreed to visit on 28th June.

Both pages: Nottingham's Quincentenary celebrations in the summer of '49 had been graced by a visit by Princess Elizabeth and the Duke of Edinburgh. Six years later the popular royal couple was back, but this time Elizabeth was our Queen. The Queen and Prince Philip had accepted an invitation to visit the Royal Agricultural Show, and of course their itinerary was planned so that the people of Nottingham had an opportunity to give them a proper Royal welcome to the city - and one of our photographs shows an enthusiastic, flag-waving crowd doing just that, as the limousines sweep up Albert Street, past Newmans. The party had travelled down from Edinburgh by rail the previous day, spending the night in the Royal coach in a siding outside Nottingham, and the train had then pulled into Nottingham Midland in the morning. This used to be the normal pattern when members of the Royal family had to travel long distances to their engagements. Presumably, sleeping in the Royal coach is a very different experience from trying to snatch a few hours' shut-eye in a third, or even first class compartment.

Certainly when the Queen and the Duke of Edinburgh alighted at Nottingham Midland - the Queen wearing a dark dress with a floral pattern, with a silk coat of Royal blue, a neat little pink-flowered hat and long white gloves, and the Duke in a pale grey suit - they showed not the slightest trace of having slept on a train. Their busy schedule for the day included an official presentation in Council House, watching a dance display by Nottingham schoolchildren on the Forest, and - as shown on our second picture - inspecting the regimental plate; escorting the Queen is, we believe, Lt Col A A Warburton, and standing next to the Duke is Major T E Forman Hardy. Later the Queen made herself useful by pressing a green button and starting up an experimental prototype high-speed lace machine, developed and displayed by John Jardine & Co Ltd. In fact most of their time in Nottingham was spent at Wollaton Park - and they were not the only royal visitors to the Royal Agricultural Show that day: the Princess Royal was there, and the Duke of Gloucester happened to be around that neck of the woods too, and popped in on an unofficial visit.

The two lads immediately behind Mr Hawksley are marching along smartly in time to the beat, but further back, little feet seem to have got somewhat out of step, and at least one little girl seems to be skipping in her excitement! The caption on our photograph informs us that Mr H Hawksley is leading the children of St Albans Street. In fact, we note that a good many of the parents of St Albans Street seem to have tagged along behind as well - and why not; coronation celebrations are for everybody to enjoy. The street is gaily decorated, and although the photograph is in black and white, we have no doubt that the bunting and the garlands were all red, white and blue. We guess that the striped hats were red, white and blue as well - and maybe even the Indian head-dress, who knows. The boys' long shorts and long socks and the little girls' frocks, worn with white ankle socks and sandals, were absolutely typical of children's dress in the 1950s. Happy smiles all round make this a thoroughly charming photograph, and one which can hardly fail to arouse nostalgia for a more neighbourly era when young and old paraded down the street, arm-in-arm, in the sunshine.

Above: The huge portrait of Queen Elizabeth II and the poster advertising the Coronation Garden Party - admission 6d - tell us plainly that this is part of the Nottingham's 1953 Coronation Carnival Procession. The parade, led by the Ruddington Silver Band, followed a five-mile route beginning and ending at the Forest. More than 50 tableaux took part, and as we can see, crowds are thronging the pavements to watch the procession as it passes through Wheeler Gate. This was just one of the stunning events which Nottingham had planned to make the Coronation a memorable and enjoyable occasion for everyone; there were fancy dress competitions, games, a Coronation Ball at the Astoria, a Coronation Pageant at Wollaton Park where 600 women joined in portraying 'Queens Through The Ages', and an open-air ballet. The participants in this latter event won everybody's admiration by going ahead in defiance of the driving rain which soaked them to the skin. The climax of the celebrations was a grand Coronation fireworks display on the Forest which lit up the sky for miles around with red, white and blue rockets. As a grand finale, fireworks shot up into the sky to create dazzling portraits of the King and Queen, which hovered above the awe-struck spectators for a few breathtaking moments. Then the spectacle slowly faded away into the night, and the applause from the 50,000-strong crowd was deafening.

On the home front

Above: This view of the waiting room at Edwards Lane clinic was one of the Health Department's contributions to the Quincentenary Local Government exhibition. Although young mums of the 21st century might not be too impressed at the idea of taking their place at the end of the row to await their turn in these rather Spartan conditions, at least the city was going to some effort to monitor the progress of its post-war babies and make sure that they grew up healthy. Each of these little bundles of joy would be taken through into the clinic's weighing room, where they would be deposited on the scales, measured, and inspected for general wholesomeness. Meanwhile the nurse's assistant would be making copious notes for the file. The birth rate was rising; many an engaged couple had decided to wait until after the war to tie the knot, and 1946 and 1947 were boom years for weddings, followed in due course by a corresponding rise in the number of babies born. The baby boom, or 'bulge', peaked around 1950, putting pressure first on baby clinics, then on schools, then on the employment market; so the social repercussions of World War II were to be much longer-lasting than many people had anticipated.

Below centre: Air raid wardens during the second world war are perhaps most famed for their keenness in spotting the least chink of light escaping through a blackout curtain. The offending householder would be startled by a sharp rap on the door and a brusque demand to 'put out that light'. In fact, air raid wardens performed many essential duties and sacrificed many a night's sleep to ensure the safety of their fellow citizens. These two air raid wardens are carrying out door-to-door gas mask inspections. One lady inspects the masks while her colleague makes notes, and the smiles suggest that all is in order in this household. After the deadly, all-pervasive mustard gas used in WW1, gas attack was perceived as a very real and terrible danger during the second world war. Millions of gas masks were manufactured before war was officially declared. Every citizen was issued with one, demonstrations were held on how to use them, and prominently-displayed posters reminded everybody to keep their

mask with them at all times. 'Hitler will send no warning - so always carry your gas mask' was one message. But as the war progressed and no gas materialised, we became somewhat more casual about gas masks. The box, if you took the mask out, made such a handy container to carry your sandwiches in . . .

Bottom: The knitting needles keep flying, the piles of packages in front of the stage keep growing, and the blackout curtain at the window confirms the likely contents and destination of those neatly-wrapped parcels. These ladies, whom we believe to be members of the Women's Auxiliary Committee of the Nottingham Boy Scouts Association, are of course knitting woollen scarves - known as comforters, or comforts - for members serving in HM Forces. As we can see, this was a highly organised operation. A special organisation called the Nottinghamshire Services Comforts Fund was established to keep everything running efficiently; and as an incentive to the knitters to keep up productivity, merit badges were issued, bearing the words 'For services rendered to our fighting men and women', and signed by H Sherwin, the Lord Mayor's secretary and honorary organiser of the Fund.

Parents always want life to be better for their children than it was for them - and that means giving them a better start in life, beginning with a better education. Each generation has its own views on what is wrong with the British educational system, and what steps should be taken to put it right. The big experiment of the 20th century was the introduction of comprehensive education. Before that, many schools had streamed pupils according to ability, but it was observed that under this system the less academically-minded were often failing to achieve their full potential. The abolition of the 11-plus examination was another milestone, which was welcomed in some spheres and condemned in others; Nottingham committed itself to

comprehensive ideals at an early stage, with non-selective senior schools featuring heavily among the new schools planned by Nottingham's Education Committee in the inter-war years. Later on, further and higher education underwent radical reform as well; immediately after the end of the second world war the government set itself the objective of raising the level of skills of the workforce, and the provision of day-release and vocational evening classes increased dramatically all over the country. Polytechnics were created, and many of these were later elevated to university status, as in the case of Nottingham Trent. Not that the youngsters seen here playing happily at Pierrepoint day nursery in the late 1940s are likely to have thought that far ahead . . .

Above: They look rather like factory workers busy in the packing department. They are in fact school teachers, preparing food parcels for children who are to be evacuated from the city - and what is immediately noticeable is the lack of young males in the photograph. The interval between conscription ending in 1920 after the first world war and starting again in anticipation of WW2 was less than 20 years, so all those who had been too young to join up first time round had their chance now; and in the Spring of 1939, call-up papers were sent to all men aged 21 and 20. The efficient organisation of the populace was essential to the country's war effort, and as the war progressed more and more people were officially called upon, either to take up arms or to register for war work. Children did their bit too, collecting scrap metal, knitting comforts for the troops, picking fruit and helping around the house. Many young lads, impatient to get into uniform, joined cadet organisations. Some became ARP messenger boys, no doubt with visions of cycling at speed, bombs landing all around them, bearing an important message that would save the nation. Even grannies were not exempt; at one stage the requirement to register for war work was extended to women aged between 46 and 50 - but of all the measures introduced by Mr Ernest Bevin, Minister of Labour and National Service, this was perhaps one of the least popular.

Right: It is often said that wartime was a time when women and girls did men's work; however, the reverse was sometimes true as well, as our photograph shows! Post-war generations have increasingly rejected the notion that boys and girls should be brought up and educated differently. Schoolboys in the 21st century are as likely to choose Home Economics as Chemistry, and many girls prefer CDT to Childcare. It may well be that the experiences of those left at home during WWII hastened this social change; the priority was to get jobs done, regardless of who did them, and many conventions had to be abandoned in the process. Even if these lads - pictured in Gotham in late 1939 or early 1940 - were not learning to knit from choice, they are certainly applying themselves to the task in hand; their little faces show intense concentration as they try to master this new skill. We do wonder whether, when these knitted comforts arrived at their destination along with many hundreds more, the troops might not have had a shrewd suspicion as to which ones were knitted by the ladies of the WVS or other women's organisations, and which were knitted by schoolboys - though we're sure the boys' contributions would have been appreciated just as much, if not more, by their recipients.

Wheels of time

I t is highly likely that many readers' first experience of banking was through the Yorkshire Penny Bank, whose branch in Clumber Street can be seen on the right of this 1955 photograph. This bank had a strong tradition of encouraging children to save. It ran a scheme whereby children could deposit their pennies with the School Transfer Department; when 240 pennies had accumulated, the pound would be transferred to a normal bank account where it would earn interest. Generations of schoolchildren joined this scheme, watched their fledgling savings grow, and grew up appreciating the benefits of saving. The bank was founded in 1856 by a successful Yorkshire businessman, Colonel Edward Akroyd, under the impressive title of the West Riding of Yorkshire Provident Society and Penny Savings Bank; the institution became simply Yorkshire Bank on 1 May 1959. Nottingham was quick to catch on to the concept of banks; the Smith's Bank, which in the mid-17th century stood in the Old Market Square, is reputed to be the first provincial bank in England. Over the years, the face of banking has changed radically. Banks' customers in days gone by used to set great store by knowing their bank manager personally; financial transactions were discussed not in a little booth with a clerk, but in the bank manager's office, which smelt of wood, leather and cigar smoke. Twenty-first century banking involves tapping numbers into the telephone, the computer or the hole-in-the-wall; few of us even know our bank manager's name.

Below: Trolley buses, like trams before them and motor buses after them, fulfilled a dual role: they took people from A to B, and they also generated a subsidiary income for the operator by acting as mobile advertisement hoardings. The apparent dearth of passengers on Nottingham Corporation's trolley bus number 454, captured by the photographer at the corner of King Street and Queen Street in August 1952 as it plied route number 36, demonstrates the importance of the second role. Trolley buses served Nottingham well for many a decade, without ever completely monopolising public road transport in the city. The changeover from electric trams to trolley buses was spread over a long period of time: trolley buses were introduced in 1927, and trams continued running until 1936. By this time Nottingham's fleet of trolley buses had reached 125, and a decade later this had risen to its peak of

157. However, by that time diesel motor buses were rapidly gaining favour, and over the next two decades trolley buses were phased out as the Corporation invested in more and more motor buses. By the time our photograph was taken nobody under the age of 16 had ever travelled by tram, and before very long trackless trams - as trolley buses used to be called - had also turned into nostalgia.

Bottom: The lens has perhaps not caught the Wilford Road bridge over the railway at its most flattering angle in, we believe, 1937; however, the elegant scrollwork on the overhead power cable supports does compensate to some degree for the rather inelegant hoardings at the side of the bridge. Near the camera, Hovis was making the most of the advertising space with a simple but witty slogan. The trade name

Hovis used to be written with the dot above the O to draw attention to its derivation. The firm was founded by Richard Smith and Thomas Fitton, who began selling their flour under the brand name of Smith's Patent Germ Flour. In 1890 they decided that a snappier name might help boost sales, and they staged a national competition, offering a prize of £25 for the best suggestion. Having worked their way through the many, many entries which flooded in, they finally awarded the prize to London student Herbert Grimes. He got Hovis from the Latin 'hominis vis', meaning 'the strength of man'. As Hovis, the company went on to become a household name; and a rather nice postscript to the story is that when Herbert died, the firm showed its appreciation by providing his widow with a pension.

Nottingham could afford to be discriminating about its railway stations in the early 20th century. The city's rail passengers were well served by trains, with four different rail companies competing for their custom: the Great Northern, Great Central, Midland, and London and North Western. Both the Midland and the Great Central operated services to London; Great Central line trains ran into Marylebone, and the Midland terminus was St Pancras, immortalised by Sir John Betjeman. In Nottingham, Victoria Station - seen on our photograph in 1953 - was the Great Central's station, also used by the Great Northern, and many people considered it to be Nottingham's finest. The facade had a pleasing symmetry and was dominated by the

great clock, which for younger readers will be practically the only recognisable thing about this photograph. Inside, beyond an oak-panelled booking hall, there was a glazed roof, numerous arches and a great deal of intricate ironwork, so the station had a spacious, open feel to it. Certainly the Great Central Railway scored points when it opened its impressive new terminus in 1900.

Four years later the Midland Railway opened a new station of its own, and although this, too, was a very fine building, somehow Victoria was always considered the better of the two, with the Midland a close runner-up. However, in the end it was the Midland which survived; Victoria was closed in September 1967, and demolition started very soon afterwards.

Bottom: Taken out of context, the sight of a woman calmly pushing her pram between two upturned juggernauts, for all the world as if this was the most normal thing to do, has a slightly surreal, Monty Python-ish feel to it. This is of course a war-time photograph, and during the war years 'normality' did tend to become somewhat distorted. In a B-movie war film, no doubt members of the Home Guard would have crouched in ambush behind the trucks, ready to open fire on the enemy as they tried to sneak into Nottingham. It was the Home Guard's job to organise the defence of cities and protect vulnerable points from Nazi attack, and they were expressly authorised to use shotguns against enemy paratroopers. The force was formed in response to an appeal by Sir Anthony Eden, Secretary of State for War, for men between 17 and 65 to form the Local Defence Volunteers. The appeal went out on 14th May, and by 27th May, Nottinghamshire had an LDV brigade 9,040 strong, of whom 3,900 were from the city of Nottingham. Although many jokes are made about the Home Guard, alias the Look, Duck and Vanish brigade, they performed excellent work all over Britain in keeping a lookout for invaders, manning anti-aircraft rocket guns, organising balloon barrages, liaising with other units, working with the regular troops - and perhaps even heaving lorries over onto their sides.

Below centre: Stoney Street used to be dominated by warehouses. Plans to alter the street layout led to a considerable amount of demolition in the mid 1960s; the vacant site formerly occupied by warehouses was made into a temporary car park, and it was at this point that many motorists looking for somewhere to park got into the habit of making a beeline for Stoney Street. Car ownership rocketed during the 60s, with the number of cars in Britain doubling from a little over

5,000,000 in 1957 to over ten million a decade later. Some of the most popular models of the 60s can be spotted on our photograph - a Ford Anglia, a Volkswagen Beetle, a Rover, a Hillman, an FB Victor . . . is it our imagination, or were the different makes and models of car more characterful and more easily recognisable in the 60s than in more recent years? With the roads filling up, it was recognised that the car park in Stoney Street was fulfilling a very useful purpose. Other plans for the street were abandoned, and in due course a major multi-storey car park development came into being, including office accommodation and stretching back as far as St Mary's Gate. This view is taken from the back of the car park, looking across Stoney Street and down a recently-widened Barker Gate towards the Ice Stadium.

Earning a crust

Above: Back in the early 1930s, Queen Victoria's view had to be temporarily intruded upon by civil engineering works which, as we understand it, were all to do with a gravitation trunk sewer, part of the main drainage system. However, we can look over the gantry and headgear to catch a glimpse of this part of Nottingham as it was in the inter-war years. One feature which strikes us immediately is the tramlines, though by the time of this photograph trams had almost run their course in Nottingham, with the service ceasing completely in 1936. Cyclists were not sorry to see them go, as the front wheel of a bicycle, once wedged in tramlines, was hard to get out - which could

be quite exciting if a tram happened to be approaching at the time. The ornate lamp standards are another nice little detail of the period. Griffin and Spalding are in what was at the time their new building, but in their time-honoured spot, and next door is the Mikado Cafe, which in 1922 had what was termed a 'springed dance floor' installed. These two businesses were to remain side by side for another three decades or so after our photograph was taken. However, by the early 1960s Griffin and Spalding had become part of the retail giant Debenhams. Debenhams then purchased the Mikado Cafe for £200,000, and soon afterwards knocked it down and expanded the store along Long Row.

All the mess and upheaval seen in this photograph from 1927 was due to the creation of a new traffic island in Theatre Square. The spectacle of the policeman standing in his box to direct the traffic reminds us that this new road layout had also entailed the removal of the statue of Samuel Morley, who used to stand here. Policemen on point duty were once a common sight. In more recent times, the police only perform this function when a set of traffic lights has gone on the blink, or when a special event is causing sudden localised congestion. But it used to be part of the bobby's job to control the traffic at busy junctions, and to see pedestrians safely across pedestrian crossings. Apparently the idea of lights to control traffic was first implemented in 1868, when a manually-operated gas lamp was used in London to allow MPs to cross the road outside the Houses of Parliament, but this was abandoned in 1872. When this photograph was taken, electric red, amber and green traffic lights at junctions were still a new phenomenon. The idea of marking out pedestrian crossings and giving them flashing beacons was not put forward until 1934, and was one of the measures introduced by Leslie Hore-Belisha to bring down the number of pedestrians killed and injured on the roads.

Below: On this photograph we see construction work in progress on Abbey Bridge in early 1927. As Nottingham's suburbia grew up around the city in the latter part of the 19th century, more roads were needed. New boulevards were created, forming in effect an early ring road around the city. Castle Boulevard was built to connect the new suburb of Lenton with the city centre; prior to that, Derby Road had been the only road from Nottingham to Lenton. Horse-drawn trams used to operate a service along this route, and part of Derby Road was so steep that the regular pair of horses was not able to pull a tram up the incline, so an additional horse had to be harnessed up to provide the extra horse power needed. Castle Boulevard offered a flatter route from Lenton to Nottingham. The city continued to spread outwards, with Wollaton Park Estate and Highfields campus and park being built during the 1920s. To serve the new conurbations, the road network spread too, and in 1927 Abbey Bridge was built as an extension to Castle Boulevard. Much later, a new road which crossed the river was built to the south of Abbey Bridge, to serve the large-scale housing development created at Clifton in the 1950s. Clifton Bridge was opened in 1958, and a further section of road was then constructed from there to Abbey Bridge, to link Clifton Boulevard with Castle Boulevard.

Bottom: If the maxim 'No hat, no boots - no job' were applied to the workers seen here employed on the widening of the LMSR bridge over Wollaton Road in 1936, then all tools would be downed in an instant. Construction workers were far more cavalier about safety measures in the first half of the 20th century. The relationship between employer and employee changed a great deal, due to a large extent to the strength of the Trades Unions in the mid-20th century, and improved health and safety at work was one of the features of the latter decades. And it was not only in the workplace that we became, as a nation, more safety conscious. Some readers who were motorcyclists in their youth will still remember the days when it was permissible to ride without a crash helmet, enjoying the wind in your hair. Seatbelts in the front seats of cars only became compulsory in the 1970s, and a massive publicity drive featuring Jimmy Saville was organised to encourage people to 'clunk, click, every trip.'

Below: Nottingham's brave firemen are seen here giving their faithful fire engines a little tender loving care. A quick glance at the engines would suggest a date somewhere around the middle of the 20th century, but in fact the photograph was taken rather later, in 1973. These three Leyland fire engines were acquired by the brigade in 1954, but having completed almost 20 years service they are now receiving their last spit and polish at the hands of Nottingham County Fire Service before being sold, along with two others. And if 20 years sounds a long time to keep a fire engine, then one of the horse-drawn fire engines used in the earlier 19th century served them for around 70 years! The town's first steam fire engine, acquired around 1864, had a one-inch diameter hose and projected water for 130 feet. Later that same decade £650 was invested in a new Shand & Mason engine which projected water to a height of 180 feet, at a rate of 400 gallons a minute. Motor fire engines came along in 1911 in the form of two six-cylinder Dennis engines, capable of delivering 800 gallons of water a minute. The Fire Brigade used to be very proud of each new acquisition, and demonstrations used to be held in the city to show just what the latest fire engine was capable of.

Right: Employees of the city's Parks Department are seen here working away with a will, putting the finishing touches to flower beds around Queen Victoria's feet four years before she departed to stand in the Memorial Gardens. The photograph is dated 24th June, 1949; on the 26th June Nottingham will launch its week of Quincentenary celebrations, so it is important for the city to look its best - especially as a Royal visit features on the agenda. Union Jacks and bunting adorn the streets, and the shop windows are full of special Quincentenary displays as traders entered into the spirit and competed for the prizes which were on offer for the best window displays. A full programme of festivities was organised for the week 26th June to 2nd July, including pageants, carnivals and sports. Only four years after the end of the war, many citizens were still rebuilding their lives, and some rationing was still in force - though clothes rationing had ended earlier that year. And, four years after Hiroshima, peace still seemed a little fragile. The Iron Curtain had fallen between East and West, and we were becoming afraid of Reds under the bed. But we must keep a sense of proportion: here, the scene is full of sunshine, flowers and citizens strolling about apparently without a care in the world.

Sowing the seeds of success

Amongst the most famous nurseries in the country is that of W.C.Wicks Ltd based at The Floralands Garden Centre, Catfoot Lane in Nottingham. The firm was founded in 1880 by William Charles Wicks. Before striking out in business on his own William Wicks had, like his father before him, been employed as a gardener; at the time he was born his parents lived in the Lodge House at Merton Hall in Surrey where his father was gardener for Lord Nelson the descendent of the great admiral. As a young man W.C. Wicks was sent away to receive his professional training at Veith's Royal Exotic Nursery, Chelsea, then the foremost nursery in England.

In 1880 W.C. Wicks opened his own business in Mapperley, Nottingham where his extensive knowledge of choice and rare plants was soon instrumental in introducing to Nottingham many decorative and flowering plants previously unknown to the district. The firm's original nurseries and greenhouses were on Querneby Road. Those premises were in use from 1880 to 1952. In the beginning the business was entirely wholesale supplying landscapers, retailers, major gardens and parks with plants, trees and shrubs.

Later the business also included a stall at the Old Market Place in Nottingham, a stall frequently patronised by Mrs Boot of Boots the Chemists fame whose purchases would have to be delivered by horse drawn tram to her home in Wilford Lane by younger members of the Wicks family. W.C. Wicks remained a familiar figure in the Nottingham market for over forty years.

W.C. Wicks' two sons the second William Wicks and his brother George James Wicks were born in the 1890s and both eventually joined the firm - they also both served in the Great War. George James, serving as a sapper in the Royal Engineers, received a bullet through his head at Gallipoli and was mentioned in despatches having his

Above left: *William Charles Wicks.*
Below: *An early picture of the staff.*

citation for 'gallant and distinguished service in the field' signed by Winston Churchill then Secretary of State for War. Despite his wounds George not only survived the war but lived until he was 81 years old.

George Wicks moved to Lambley with his wife Florence May in 1923 when the Old Nursery at Lambley was purchased. At that time a few greenhouses were the only things standing on the site - fortunately there was a well and so irrigation was soon installed.

Times were far from easy. In the 1930s during the great depression the family struggled to build up the business at Lambley, 'making something from nothing' as George would recall in his old age. And of course things changed significantly on the outbreak of the second world war.

During the war 90 per cent of all the firm's ornamental nursery stock was replaced by food crops. Most of the young men who had worked for the firm went off to war leaving only one or two men and fifteen land girls, recruited mostly from local teenagers, to keep the business functioning. Towards the end of the war in 1944, in his ninetieth year, and after an illness lasting only a few days William C.Wicks, the firm's founder, passed on. His death came just a year after that of his wife Elizabeth whom he had married at St Nicholas' church in 1878 . Those who

knew him would always remember him as one of the leading authorities in horticulture in the Midlands.

In 1947, not long after the end of hostilities, one of W.C. Wicks' grandsons, another George Wicks, opened a flower shop in Bridlesmith Gate Nottingham; sadly that branch of the family business closed in 1980. Other family members however remained in the business: despite his war injuries George James Wicks had joined the company, working his way up from the bottom and had soon gained a reputation for being hardworking, honest and charitable - and eventually for expecting those around him to observe the same standards. Today it is George's son James Anthony (Tony) Wicks who is now the family patriarch.

Like his father before him Tony Wicks also joined the company as a young man but at the age of fifteen was

Above left: George James Wicks' citation from the first world war. **Top:** *An early market scene.* **Below:** *Workers in the 1920s.*

first sent away from home to work at a nursery in Huddersfield called Blackburns ; he stayed there for two years before volunteering to join the army at the outbreak of war. During the second world war Tony served in the Royal Irish Fusiliers. Coming out of the army he joined the business working for his father George who by that time was growing a varied range of ornamental pot plants - famously the firm had been the first to market poinsettias and azaleas in Nottingham.

It was however 1957 which was to be remembered as the year the firm arrived at the top of the horticultural profession. That story began six years earlier in 1951 when the business had taken delivery of a dozen or so shabby looking African Violets, sun scalded but with an odd bloom or two on them. After buying several books on caring for African Violets and making further imports of stock from California sales of the new plants began in 1952. The firm set out its first display of the African Violets at the Royal Horticultural Society's hall in London on 15 th June 1954 and was awarded the Society's Silver Flora Medal. The following year the firm gained another silver medal at the Chelsea Flower Show at which their display was visited by the Queen Mother. The feat was repeated in the following year when the firm received its first gold medal. It was though in 1957 that the firm reached the pinnacle of professional recognition with no fewer than six gold medals awarded at six consecutive flower shows . Wicks' African Violets (Saint Paulia) were to affect national trends in fashion, makeup and colour schemes.

Right: Loading up in the 1940s.
Below: Four generations of the Wicks family in a picture taken at the Yews in 1937.

The awards gained by the firm became as much a selling point as its practical experience of growing African violets. Being the first nursery to grow these plants commercially, crowds of people would converge on the firm's stand at shows clamouring to buy them. The firm continued to exhibit at Chelsea until the mid 1970s.

The 1970s were a decade of change. George had passed on in 1973 though he had remained involved in the company until the very last. Change was needed. George had been dubious about doing business on a Sunday but the greenhouses were failing with high fuel bills and dilapidated timbers. At the time the business had two and a half acres of greenhouses, forty acres of trees and shrubs and employed about thirty people. In 1979 Tony Wicks took the difficult decision to bulldoze the greenhouses and, with deep regret, to make twenty nursery staff redundant keeping only seven on.

Those who remained included Philip Frost then the firm's specialist camellia and clematis grower and now the firm's general manager and a director of the company. Chris Philips now the firm's

shrub and tree manager, then working in the houseplant department, was also kept on.

In 1979 Tony's vision had been to build a greenhouse that opened its doors at weekends to the passing public - but as his father George had often said to him 'If your grandfather was here he would tell you if you can't make the business work in six days you are in the wrong business'.

It took slightly longer than six days to make the new venture work but Tony Wicks' vision was to prove to be fully justified. Today the firm employs eight full time and a large number of part time staff.

Sadly Tony's son Christopher Nigel Wicks who wanted to carry on the company was tragically killed in an accident in December 1992 aged 28: - 'Who plucked this flower? I, said the master'. Christopher's younger brother Gregory Neil Wicks and their sister Sonya Gail Wicks have gone in other directions along life's path.

Today business is buoyant: main sales in the UK are to the general public who love plants, flowers and gardens and flock to buy all the products and services associated with this large garden centre. The firm puts its popularity down to its technical superiority the result of many, many years of horticultural experience.

As Tony Wicks says 'we always try our very best to help people and if on the odd occasion we make a mistake, well as Ruskin said "he who never made a mistake never made anything".'

In the spring of the year 2000, the company embarked on upon an ambitious development

programme to include a restaurant (with seating for 100 people), an undercover plant market, and a large outdoor landscaped area for a larger range of big ornamental trees and shrubs with many being imported from abroad.

After some 30 years these changes will be signalled by a new name 'The Floralands Garden Village'. Looking to the distant future, the first tree (a weeping copper beech) was planted to mark the inauguration of the 'Floralands Lambley Museum Arboretum' which will in time, it is hoped, provide for people a peaceful sanctuary where beauty and tranquility may abound to help relieve the modern day pressures that are endured by most.

Top: *Lambley Nurseries from the air in 1938.*
Below: *Tony Wicks (centre) plants the first specimen in the Millennium Arboretum with John Stirland (left) and Martin Fish.*

On the right road for over 40 years

The Willoughby family members are no fools. Even though their garage business first saw the light of day on 1 April 1960, from the very beginning it was no joke for its competitors. Willoughby Garages soon developed a formidable reputation for reliable and efficient service. In the world of the motor trade this is not easy to achieve. There have been times when the press has been unkind to car dealers and garages. Whilst in some cases this might have been justified, the name of Willoughby has shone out proudly for all that is best in this field. As a family concern, it has served its customers well for over 40 years. A steady supply of regulars has stayed faithful to the company through those times. They have been more than happy with what has been on offer and Willoughby's is rightly proud of its record and reputation. It is a local company meeting local needs.

Jack Keith Willoughby and his brother, Rex William, established the company with the financial backing of their father, William Lawrence. He was a civil engineering contractor who was involved in open cast coal mining and playing field development around Ilkeston. William wanted to move into the business sector and the interests of his sons provided the perfect outlet for his ambitions. Both were avid motor enthusiasts. Jack was a keen rally driver and Rex was pursuing an interest in racing cars. They were able to combine their passion with skills ideally suited to the motor trade. As well as bringing ideas to the company, they had an added advantage over their competitors. They knew cars inside out. Rex was a qualified mechanic, so his knowledge had a formal basis as well as the practical side he had picked up from his close association with racing. Jack also had more to offer than his obvious know-how about motors. He was a university graduate who had been articled to an accountant. With such a wealth of talent at its disposal it would have been a surprise if Willoughby's had done anything else other than develop rapidly.

In the early days the company was known as WL Willoughby, using the father's name as its title. The business was formed by purchasing premises on Wollaton Road in Beeston, where Willoughby Garages can still be found today. Leslie Jackson had run Beeston Light Car Company on this site since the end of World War II. In the 1930s it had been an ambulance station, so the ground was well used to seeing the wheels of business turning over it. When the Willoughbys bought Mr Jackson's premises they took on the 20 or so employees he had as part of the package. The fact that their jobs were safeguarded promoted a sense of loyalty in the workforce that is still apparent today. The firm places great store by good will and this is evident in abundance from employees and customers alike.

Below: The garage forecourt pictured in the 1950s.

The 1960s was a good time to get into the garage business. The whole country was facing a period of economic growth. Unemployment was low and people had money in their pockets to spend on items that had once been luxuries, but soon were to become commonplace possessions. Even the Prime Minister, Harold Macmillan, had, as the 1950s drew to a close, trumpeted that the electorate 'had never had it so good'. Alec Issigonis' Mini had been launched in 1959 and Britain was well on its way to becoming a nation of motorists. Cheaper, but reliable, cars came within the reach of ordinary people. Willoughby's was ready to feed the boom that was coming. Within a few short years further premises were acquired in Ilkeston. These were William Willoughby's old plant yard. They were used as a second hand car dealership until 1965 when the site was sold to Kenning's, but development did not end there. By the mid 60s there was Redhill Garage, Mansfield, that sold Fords. Frank Nicholson's Chilwell garage was also taken under the Willoughby wing. Frank was a member of the old school of businessmen. He was so wrapped up in his world that three months after selling out he was still coming on almost daily to open the post! In keeping with the Willoughby philosophy, babies were not thrown out with the bath water. Recognising that new brooms need to be selective where they clean, the talents of Peter Quemby were recognised.

Above: *The automatic carwash in the 1960s.*
Top: *The shape of things to come - the advent of the self service petrol station in the early 1970s.*

He had been Nicholson's office manager for over 20 years. He was retained and promoted to branch manager until 1990. Peter rose to become one of the company directors and his daughter, Tricia, continues the Quemby link by also working for Willoughby's. Her husband, John Allum joined the Chilwell garage from the Navy. Today he is another of the company's directors.

Many of the company's employees have been with the firm for over 25 years and have shared in the development from one garage to many outlets in and around the Nottingham area. These have included leases taken on several Mobil garages, such as Elms Park, Loughborough, where a small service bay was attached, and the Broadgate garage in Bramcote Lane, Wollaton. Mobil complimented Willoughby's by awarding it 'best kept station' accolades on a number of occasions. However, the Mobil connection was severed in 1985 when the company transferred to supplying Esso.

It was Jack Willoughby who was the guiding light for most of the business success. Rex left in 1968 to pursue an independent career as a property developer, so it was left to his brother to steer the family concern through to its current position as a market leader. As a 61 year old he decided to retire in 1997, but was secure in the knowledge that the company was in safe family hands. Stephen joined in 1992 after practising as a solicitor. His passion for cars and the opportunity to join the family Company proved irresistible. Caroline, a former Lloyds Bank manager, moved into the company from the banking world in 1990. Their mixture of legal and financial knowledge is a bonus in the world of big business in which Willoughby's now moves. It has maintained its position at the forefront of the business by a smart mixture of stability and innovation. It stayed with BMC, British Leyland, Triumph, Austin and Rover for over 35 years. It had the Rootes franchise, via the old connection with Frank Nicholson. As tastes and demands changed, Willoughby's was able to meet them.

Below: *A pristine showroom in the late 1960s.*
Bottom: *The original Nicholson's Garage, now demolished to make room for a modern used car centre.*

Willoughby Garages was happy to celebrate 40 years in the trade in 2000. There was a staff party and barbecue, with the Beeston Pipe Band in proud attendance. The event was big enough to be featured on Radio Trent. Customers shared in the fun. For the anniversary day petrol was sold at 5.2p per litre for every 40th customer. This works out at about 24p per gallon. Who can remember when petrol was less than five bob a gallon? One customer did well for himself by getting the equivalent of £35 worth for just a couple of pounds. However, staff are still trying to work out why one driver insisted that he only wanted about half a gallon putting in his tank. He spent less than 15p on the transaction. Talk of looking a gift horse etc!

Peugeot appeared at Chilwell in 1990, with Seat coming along in 1997. New premises were built there as the site was expanded and developed. The Peugeot connection was extended to Beeston in 1996.

Willoughby's has only failed in one aspect. It has failed to stand still. When the Green Shield stamps of the 1960s appeared, the company was among the first to use these promotional tools to attract business. The Esso price watch scheme of the late 1990s was an effective tool in raising sales and there are no prizes for guessing which garage firm supported it vigorously. Nor has Willoughby Garages ignored other aspects of development. It was the second Nottingham garage to have an automatic car wash and one of the first to have a self service forecourt, as it did in 1965. It diversified its interests with the Beeston Light Car Company driving school and by undertaking increased insurance work. Willoughby's is not standing still in the new millennium either. Recently a state-of-the-art paint bath has been installed as well as a brand new car wash and Express Fit facility. Willoughby Garages are also one of the leading car retailers on the Internet with two dedicated sites.

Top: *The Peugeot site - year 2000.*
Above left: *Some of Willoughby's longest serving employees - nearly 100 years of service between them.* **Below:** *Celebrating the delivery of the 1000th new Peugeot.*

John Player's - a special story

When in 1901 the head of the American Tobacco Company James Buchanan Duke burst in upon the Player brothers in Nottingham he did so with the words 'Hello boys; I'm Duke from New York, I've come to take over your business'. Duke could speak with some confidence: ATC had armed him with a war chest of $30 million to buy up each of Britain's major tobacco firms. Duke had already snapped up the Liverpool firm of Ogden's.

James Duke however found himself out-manoeuvred in the 'Tobacco War'. In the face of the external threat, 13 of Britain's leading tobacco firms, including Nottingham's very own Player's, merged their businesses. On 10 December 1901 the Imperial Tobacco Company (of Great Britain and Ireland) was formed. Only when Imperial Tobacco threatened Duke on his own turf did he offer a truce and end the war.

For residents of Nottingham however, the face of the Imperial Tobacco Group will forever be Player's. John Player and Sons was founded by John Player in 1877. The son of a solicitor from Saffron Walden in Essex, John Player came to Nottingham in 1862 just six years after the first cigarette factory in Britain had been opened at Walworth in London in 1856 by Robert Peacock Gloag.

Top left: John Player, founder of the firm. ***Top right:*** *James Buchanan Duke, who made an early attempt to buy out the company.*
Above centre: *The famous Player's logo.*
Below and facing page: *Early advertisements and cards for Player's products.*

PLAYER'S CIGARETTES

PRODUCTS OF THE WORLD.

ONE OF INTERESTING THESE PICTURES
IS NOW BEING ISSUED IN EVERY PACKET OF
PLAYER'S NAVY CUT CIGARETTES.

JOHN PLAYER & SONS, Castle Tobacco Factory. NOTTINGHAM.

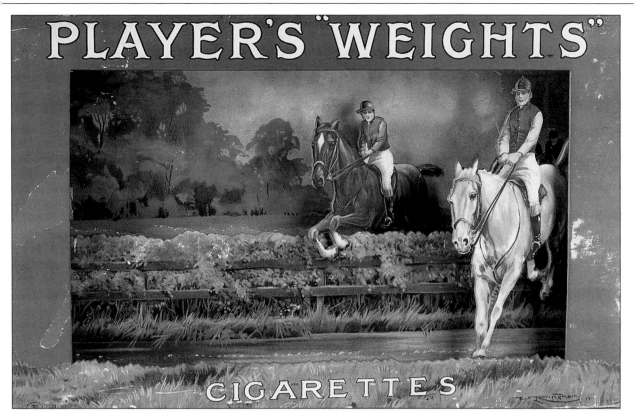

John Player tried his hand at being a draper's assistant before leaving that trade to set up shop on Beastmarket Hill as an agent of Prentice and Co's agricultural manures and seeds. At that time tobacco was sold loose from jars, and even hand-made cigarettes were weighed out on scales according to individual need. John began buying loose tobacco and selling it as a side-line, probably in 'screws', costing a few pence each. From this it was a logical step to cater for a customer's regular demand for a certain brand of tobacco by pre-packaging it. The side-line took over and the shop prospered.

Fifteen years after his arrival in Nottingham John Player acquired a small tobacco manufacturing business in Broad Marsh. The business, producing pipe and chewing tobaccos as well as hand-made cigarettes, had been established in 1823 by one William Wright and at the time of its sale to John Player employed about 150 workers. The first Player's trade mark - a drawing of Nottingham Castle - first appeared in

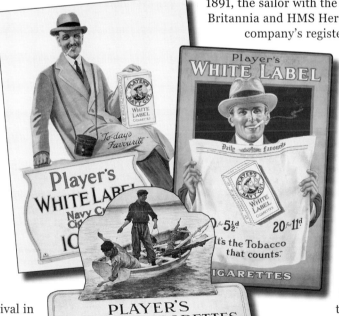

1877. The famous Player's sailor's head took shape more gradually, first the sailor himself was registered in 1883, then five years later the lifebouy frame with Player's Navy Cut superimposed and, in 1891, the sailor with the two ships HMS Britannia and HMS Hero became the company's registered trademark.

Contrary to popular belief, the sailor's head does not represent any particular individual, but was simply an artist's conception.

John Player's marketing methods were so effective that by 1881 he purchased an extensive site at Radford where, with considerable foresight, he proceeded to build three factory blocks, the nucleus of the 30 acres of factories and offices which were eventually to grow on the site. At the time he needed only one of the blocks; the other two he leased to lace manufacturers until such time as they might be needed for his expansion - an event which was to occur in the closing years of the 19th century though only after the last lace maker had his steam cut off and was taken to the Nottingham Assizes.

Sadly John Player died aged only 45 in 1884 - the year in which the first of the Radford blocks, the Castle Tobacco Factory, was opened. The business continued its expansion however, managed by a group of close friends, until John Player's sons, John Dane Player and William Goodacre Player, were able to take over as managing directors in 1893.

In 1895 the firm became a private limited company and by 1898 all three blocks were in operation as tobacco factories. Working conditions were given a high priority and John Player's involvement with the welfare of its employees was reflected both in the progressive work practices and conditions found in the firm's factories.

Player's Gold Leaf Navy Cut Cigarettes were well established before 1890; they were the forerunners of the famous Player's Medium Navy Cut Cigarettes introduced before the turn of the century.

By then five 'Elliott' machines were being used, each capable of turning out 200 cigarettes a minute; in addition some 200 girls widely known as 'Player's Angels' were making cigarettes by hand, the most efficient making 2,000 per day.

By the time the new factories became operational the firm was employing 1,000 workers and by 1914 so much expansion had taken place that 2,500 people were being employed at Radford.

During the first world war Players cigarette cards, now collectors' items, became extremely popular. The cards, originally used as stiffeners in paper packets, first appeared in the USA before 1880 although the first British manufacturer did not issue one until

LIGHT UP THIS MOMENT WITH
BACHELOR TIPPED

PLAYER'S BACHELOR TIPPED
The tip for smart people

1887. The early series of Player's cards, issued during the Boer War period, included two sets of Actresses and several military sets. Typical titles from the first world war period include 'Artillery in Action', 'Regimental Uniforms', 'Colonial and Indian Army Badges'. 'War Trophies' and a series on Napoleon and his campaigns.

In 1926 the Player brothers retired from active participation in the business. Their gifts to charity were on a princely scale and yet, so shy were they of publicity, the exact amount of their benefactions may never be known. John D Player did however give generously towards rebuilding the Children's Hospital, the General Hospital, convalescent homes, local churches and schools - particularly the High School which the brothers had both attended. William G Player gave over £150,000 towards a nurses' home and made lavish contributions to local churches.

Ironically the Chancellor of the Exchequer was the greatest beneficiary on the death of the Player brothers. On John D Player's death in 1950 one newspaper said 'It took John Player 70 years to amass his fortune; it took Sir Stafford Cripps but a moment to take nearly £2,000,000 of it'. John D Player was 85 when he died; his brother William 93. The young men who had once shown James Duke the door had had quite a long innings.

The factory buildings originally completed in 1884 were added to several times over the years to provide a huge complex. The main periods of expansion can be identified: 1910-14, 1920-22, 1926-32 and 1939-40 when two more factories and a bonded warehouse were built.

Above: *Two advertisements, the top one from the 1950s and the bottom one from the 1940s.*

Some idea of the rapid strides made by Player's can be gathered from the steadily increasing number of employees - 2,500 in 1914 and 7,500 in 1939.

During the second world war other additions were made to the site. Under No 1 factory an air raid tunnel 3,000 feet long was constructed 30 feet underground which could provide accommodation for 3,000 people. Fortunately it never had to be used in earnest.

By 1960 the year of the Diamond Jubilee of Player's Navy Cut the company was riding a wave of success. It was in 1962 that the John Player Trophy for show jumping was inaugurated and won by Harvey Smith, Since then few people can have missed the important connection between the John Player name and sponsorship a field pioneered in the UK by Players and a handful of other major companies - motor racing, motor cycle racing, rugby, cricket and the arts have all found a place on the sponsorship list.

Above: *The JPS sponsored motorcycle.*
Right: *The Ultra High Speed making and packing complex.*
Below: *Player's Nottingham premises today.*

In 1966 Player's launched its first coupon brand Player's No 6 which became an overnight winner, and soon became the country's top selling brand.

The biggest ever addition to John Player's operation came in 1972 with the opening of the £14 million Horizon factory occupying a 45 acre site at Lenton. It was the most modern factory of its kind in the world, attracting international interest and acclaim.

Over recent years the company has invested heavily in the Horizon factory, equipping it with the latest technology and developing innovative new processing techniques. Imperial Tobacco's cigarette brands for the UK and export markets are manufactured at the Nottingham site and today the company's ultra-high-speed making and packing complexes are capable of producing 14,000 cigarettes per minute. Horizon's total production capacity will soon stand at over 55 billion cigarettes a year.

Overseas sales now account for 45 per cent of company profits and as a result of growing cigarette export volumes, the manufacture of roll-your-own tobacco has been transferred from Nottingham to Liverpool and Mullingar, allowing for a number of new mid-speed cigarette machines to be installed. Imperial is now one of the world's lowest cost producers of quality tobacco products - all a far cry from those distant days in the 1870s when John Player first sold tobacco as a side-line in his agricultural products shop.

Nottingham Building Society - a proud tradition of putting people first

Since 1849, Nottingham Building Society has had a proud tradition of putting its customers first. The principles of the founders were to promote the culture of home ownership whilst providing a safe haven for savings. Over 150 years later, these ideals have helped The Nottingham grow to become a top 20 building society and influence why it intends remaining a traditional building society.

The Nottingham is a community-based building society committed to the region it serves. The Society's Community Awards scheme and Sports Sponsorship programme assist over 200 local groups and organisations each year. A wide range of projects receive support including many related to education, the environment, health, crime reduction and debt counselling. Many clubs which received Sports Sponsorship awards would not have survived without The Nottingham's support.

With a network of branches in Nottinghamshire, Derbyshire, Lincolnshire and South Yorkshire, Nottingham Building Society is one of the most successful regional building societies in the UK.

People of vision

In 1849, a group of people with vision and integrity formed Nottingham Building Society to 'promote the construction of a better class of dwellings, suitable for the middle and working classes, and also to provide a profitable and safe place for small savings.' They were led by 68 year old Samuel Fox (1781 - 1868), a leading Quaker and prominent local grocer. He was a generous man who was involved with every philanthropic activity in the town.

Groceries and savings accounts

In 1858, The Nottingham moved from George Street, Nottingham to the grocer's shop of Samuel Fox in High Street Place, Nottingham. So, Nottingham Building Society was offering a combination of groceries and savings accounts nearly 150 years ago - long before supermarkets came on the scene! When Samuel Fox stepped down as chairman at the grand age of eighty in 1861, the Society moved to 16 Fletcher Gate, Nottingham and opened daily.

"Bank Of England Governor opens new building society offices"

This was the headline in the Nottingham Journal's edition of 29 September 1929. Engaging Sir Josiah Stamp, governor of the Bank of England at the time, to unlock the doors of the new chief office was certainly a triumph for The Nottingham. During 1998, those same historic offices in Friar Lane, Nottingham were given a complete facelift and were re-opened by the Sheriff of Nottingham, Councillor Chris Gibson.

The war years

During the second world war Nottingham suffered from enemy air raids but to a lesser extent than many cities of comparable size. A major air raid on the city occurred on the night of 8 May 1941 and among the buildings destroyed were several at the south-eastern corner of Friar Lane in the centre

Above: *Sir Josiah Stamp, Governor of the Bank of England, opens the new Friar Lane offices in 1929.*
Below: *Nottingham Market Place, Nottingham 1859. Print courtesy of Nottingham City Council: Leisure and Community Services, Angel Row Library.*

Expansion in the seventies

The Annual Report for 1974 announced the acquisition of 5-13 Upper Parliament Street which became The Nottingham's head office in 1975. During the seventies, new branch offices were opened in over 35 locations including Beeston, Arnold, Long Eaton, Mansfield, Skegness, Chesterfield and Sheffield.

Innovation in the eighties

One of the highlights of Nottingham Building Society's progress in the eighties was the arrival in 1983 of Britain's first electronic home banking service through a joint venture with Prestel, then British Telecom's computerised information system. Ahead of its time, it pioneered electronic interaction

Above: Nottingham Building Society's hot air balloon, The Flying Cottage. **Top:** *The Nottingham's Friar Lane offices in 1929.* **Right:** *Nottingham Building Society's interactive internet site was launched in 1998 at the Tales of Robin Hood tourist attraction in Nottingham. The Nottingham, well known for its eye catching Robin Hood logo, officially launched the site with the help of the real Sheriff of Nottingham, Councillor Tony Robinson. Pictured at the launch from left to right are: Little John (Matthew Allen), Stuart Brandreth, managing director of Nottingham Building Society and Councillor Tony Robinson, the Sheriff of Nottingham.*

of Nottingham. Except for minor blast damage, Nottingham Building Society's offices, situated just 50 yards away, escaped virtually unscathed.

between the building society and its customers. On 14 February 1981, The Nottingham's hot air balloon, the Flying Cottage made its maiden flight. The yellow balloon in the shape of a cottage was a popular attraction and was regularly seen flying in the sky over Nottingham, or featured at many special events.

Birth of Nottingham Property Services

The 1986 Building Societies Act extended the range of services that building societies could provide. Societies could establish estate agencies, offer insurance services and provide unsecured loans. In 1989, Nottingham Building Society launched a residential estate agency known as Nottingham Property Services. Today, Nottingham Property Services has 19 branches and has grown to be a leading estate agency in its trading area.

And the success continues...

Nottingham Building Society ended the twentieth century having achieved record results. The Society now has almost 200,000 customers and total assets of £1.4 billion. Its internet website (www.nottingham-bs.co.uk) provides up to the minute information about mortgages and savings and its interactive facility enables people to work out example repayments and obtain information on the local interest rates.

As a new millennium dawns, Nottingham Building Society's pledge is to deliver long term value for money through competitive rates and quality service, for many years to come.

Enhancing homes for over 100 years

Times were hard in the long-ago days when Frank Edwin Hopewell started selling second hand furniture. It was the late 19th century, and the ambitious young man had no capital, no business experience, no further education and no qualifications. But he did have determination and the willingness to work hard, and he put his heart and soul into his little shop in Great Alfred Street.

In 1890 Frank Edwin married Annie Elizabeth Buxton, and he was destined to find that two could not live as cheaply as one. Their first child, also named Frank, soon came along and was followed at regular intervals by Ernest, Jim, Edith, Bernard, Connie, Claude and Eric, and the young couple and their children found themselves living, at times, a hand to mouth existence. Yet even though on occasions they had no idea where their next meal was coming from, Annie Hopewell took many of the local children under her wing, feeding them, giving them a bath, and kitting them out in fresh clothes. Annie was a remarkable young woman with the ability not only to run a home and bring up a family, but with a business

sense that was unusual among women at the time - and her strong personality made her well-respected among her husband's staff.

Frank Hopewell was a young man of high principles, and though life remained a desperate struggle for a number of years, he never failed to meet his obligations and his scrupulous honesty earned him the trust of his suppliers. One well-remembered weekend found him with no funds in the bank and an outstanding bill to pay on Monday morning. His solution was to load up a dray with furniture from the shop, drive the 16 miles to Mansfield, and auction off his stock in the market place. Needless to say, the bill was paid promptly as the bank opened on Monday morning.

As finances began to improve, moves were made to larger premises, first to a nearby shop in Great Alfred Street, then in 1898 to 176 St Ann's Well Road, and later to a

*Above left: The Hopewell family in 1906. **Below:** The shop on St Ann's Well Road with Frank Edwin Hopewell in the foreground.*

double fronted shop at numbers 156 and 158 St Ann's Well Road, where they were able to announce that they had the largest furniture showroom in Nottingham. By the 1920s a branch of the store was opened at Radford Road. As with many most furniture businesses, Hopewell's developed a removals business which flourished side by side with furniture sales and eventually became the largest removals firm in Nottingham.

By the 1930s the business had become very successful, and Ernest, Jim, Bernard, Claude and Eric were all involved with the family firm. Frank, the eldest son, had sadly died in his teens, and now tragedy was poised to strike at the heart of the family once more. In 1936 the firm's founder, Frank Edwin, was killed in a car accident.

Three years later the country was at war with Germany, and Hopewell's found themselves once more in a tight corner. One by one the staff left to serve in the forces or to become involved in war work, and Bernard was left to carry on as best he could with a much reduced staff. Furnishing was a difficult business to be involved in during the war years; at first no new furniture was made at all, then the Utility Furniture Scheme was introduced, providing for only a limited number of pieces of furniture to be purchased by newly married couples. The large stock of furniture already held in Hopewell's showroom, coupled with the amount of storage space which was much in demand during the war, helped the firm to survive.

When the war ended in 1945 Eric and later Claude, were able to return to the business, joined later by Eric's son John. Gradually war time restrictions were lifted, utility furniture was phased out, and the Hopewells and their staff could breathe a sigh of relief and put their minds to

developing the business. The proposed compulsory purchase of the premises by the Corporation for the building of a large roundabout led to the acquisition of the nearby Burton building; the roundabout plans were eventually abandoned, leaving Hopewell's with premises on both sides of Parliament Street.

The 1960s and 70s saw further expansion and development, modernisation and innovation. Branch shops were opened in Leicester and Derby - though in 1983 the store in Leicester was destroyed by fire. The Nottingham and Derby stores continued to flourish. Today, under the guidance of Bernard's son Gordon, John and his son Adam, Hopewell's continues to go from strength to strength, offering their customers both a high standard of service and tasteful furnishings that will enhance their homes and give lasting pleasure and satisfaction for many years to come.

Above: Parliament Street and Milton Street premises in the 1950s. Below: The Huntingdon Street premises built in 1973.

John E Wright & Co Ltd - quality, service and stability in changing times

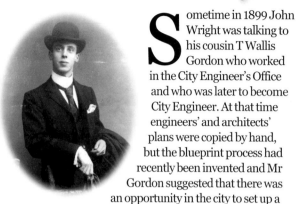

Sometime in 1899 John Wright was talking to his cousin T Wallis Gordon who worked in the City Engineer's Office and who was later to become City Engineer. At that time engineers' and architects' plans were copied by hand, but the blueprint process had recently been invented and Mr Gordon suggested that there was an opportunity in the city to set up a business for copying plans in this way.

John Wright took up the challenge and in March 1900 bought his first machine. The blueprint process involves exposing a piece of paper, suitably chemically coated, to uv light, the only sources of which at that time were sunlight and arc lamps. A tracing of the plan to be copied was placed over the sensitised paper and the light shone on to it. Where the light struck the chemicals on the paper they changed, so that on washing with water and dilute bichromate solution they formed prussian blue. In the shadow of the lines on the tracing, the paper was unaffected and stayed white. So a blueprint is a white image on a blue ground. John Wright used both his machine, similar to the one illustrated, and sunframes which were much quicker on suitable days.

It is very difficult starting a new business, particularly where new technology is involved and the architects and engineers of the day were reluctant to give up hand copying.

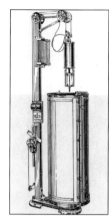

The accounts for the year 1900 survive and show that he started the year with £76 and finished with £50 13s 7d. His 1900 diary shows many days of 'nothing to do'. It must then have seemed over-optimistic to think that this business would still be thriving 100 years later.

Things must have improved, however, because he married in 1902 and with his new wife moved to a shop where he also sold the materials that architects and engineers required, drawing instruments, pens, inks, papers and pencils. He also sold water colours because at that time, as now, elevations and perspectives were often tinted. The white lines of the blueprints could also be tinted to show different services. Essentially the business was now defined, and today John E. Wright and Company Ltd. still cater for the same customers.

John Wright worked at Chilwell Depot during the first world war and at that time his elder daughter Janet started to work in the business, although only a schoolgirl, and remained a director until her death in 1999. Her married name was Janet Barnett. In 1933 Harold Crew, her brother-in-law, joined the Company.

Top left: John Wright in 1898. Top right: An early arc-lamp machine. Below left: A late arc-lamp machine (about 1940). Below right: 29 Forman Street decorated for the Coronation in 1953.

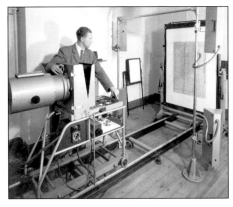

In the early 1990s the digital revolution started. First the commercial artists turned to the computer and no longer needed the graphic art materials, but they still needed proofs in accurate colour, and at first they could not do this themselves. Colour printing services are now a mixture of copying from paper copies and computer with large sizes a speciality. Copies can be encapsulated and mounted. The shop has continued to stock art materials and is now a Winsor & Newton Premier Art Centre and a Daler Rowney Main Dealer and the experienced staff cater for both the professional and amateur artist.

In 1929 the business moved to premises over the Blue Bell in Forman Street where it remained until 1963. After the war premises were also rented in Carrington Street in the basement of Stead and Simpson. This freed space in Forman Street for new photographic processes which allowed plans to be copied at a different scale to that of the original drawing. Using half plate negatives, photography also provided a convenient way of archiving drawings and many of the historic plans and maps in the County Library have been preserved in this way.

In the early 1960s the original premises had become too small and the Company acquired the site of the old St Mark's Church Hall on Huntingdon Street and erected the present building, moving in 1963. Soon after, the third generation joined the business, John Wilkinson, married to John Wright's grand-daughter, and his grandson John Barnett. The main copying process was then the diazo or dyeline process, but the first Xerox machines were on the market and the Company became one of the first 'copyshops' in Nottingham. Today all black and white copies are made by the xerographic process.

At this time a third major customer group was added. Until the 1960s all lettering was done by hand either freehand or with the use of a stencil. In about 1970 Letraset dry transfer lettering was invented, sheets of letters which could be rubbed down on to a drawing to give a much more 'professional' look. This product was seized on by the new graphic arts industry which prepared by hand the artwork for the rapidly growing advertising industry. Graphic artists used paints (mainly gouache), brushes, special high quality papers and board, special colour matched markers, and above all, Letraset. In Nottingham, John E. Wright and Co supplied them.

In the 1980s the first colour copiers were invented and the Company was among the first to offer a colour copying service in Nottingham. Also at this time the company expanded by acquiring branches in Leicester, Derby and Coventry, giving effective coverage over the East Midlands.

Architects and engineers were slower to take to the computer, but by the end of the decade most of them were using CAD packages to produce plans. This was sensible for new projects, but not so good if old plans were to be modified. This problem led to a new service of scanning plans and converting them to usable electronic data.

The arrival of the computer was coincident with the arrival of the fourth generation, Tony Barnett, now Managing Director. The digital revolution has transformed the Company on the production side, but architectural and engineering customers still have their original requirements. They want copies of large plans, even if now sent by e-mail, scale changes, and archiving - now 600 drawings on a CD-ROM rather than 600 half plates. Commercial artists need colour matched copies, colour posters, exhibition stands etc. All of these are produced digitally.

In summary the digital revolution has changed the methods but not the fundamental requirements of the community the Company serves now, and hopes to serve for another century.

Top left: *The shop counter, Forman Street in 1960.*
Top right: *The Statfile Camera - 1960.*
Right: *Dyeline printing in 1983.*

Picturing Britain

Looking for a photograph? The British Geological Survey in Keyworth houses the National Archive of Geological Photographs which contains more than 100,000 images dedicated to the earth sciences. 22,000 of those images are on fragile glass plate negatives. The archive is part of the BGS's photographic services department which, since its creation over a century ago, has supported the scientific work of the Survey. The NAGP has one of the best collections of geological pictures in the world and is certainly one of the oldest - but how did it all begin?

The photographic revolution which swept the world in the 19th century was in many respects comparable to the information technology revolution of today. It is no wonder that the Director of the Geological Survey of Great Britain at that time, Archibald Gelkie, decided that he would embrace the new technology.

In 1891, under the direction of Survey geologist Jethro Justinian Harris Teall, Mr A MacConachie, the assistant curator of the Survey collections, and

Mr Robert Lunn a general assistant in the Edinburgh office were sent to the north-west Scottish Highlands to take a series of photographs to 'help explain points of geological structure'. That first official photographic survey lasted several weeks and used a wooden field camera and tripod with glass plate negatives.

Gradually Survey geologists became interested in the benefits the technology offered in the recording describing and archiving of their work. By 1904, chiefly due to the continuing work of Robert Lunn, the Survey had begun to assemble an official picture collection.

Left: Castle Crag, Nottingham, 1907.
Below: Ironstone workings, Wartnaby, Leics. 1907. ***Bottom:*** *Lime Street Quarry, East Kirkby, Notts. 1930.*

and side-car which must have made life easier and finally, by 1945, he had use of a motor car.

Today the BGS is experiencing another technical revolution with computers now part of the photographer's equipment.

The first officially catalogued image in the collection is an English picture entitled 'Puddle Trench for Howden Reservoir, Derbyshire'. The picture was taken in 1904 on glass quarter plate by J J H Teall, by then Director of the Survey.

One of the finest underground mining photographers was John Charles Burrows who took a series of glass plates documenting the Cornish tin mines in 1891. Burrows was friend of William Thomas of the Cambourne Mining School who encouraged him to publish several of his plates in a book 'Mongst Mines and Miners' (1893). They were printed in sepia and it was that book which gained Burrows the first mining fellowship of the Royal Photographic Society.

Two photographers very prominent in the Survey's early English photographic collections were Thomas Clifford Fitzwilliam Hall and Donald Alexander MacAlister. Both those men were mining geologists and Hall was charged with photography within the Survey's English division.

Hall and MacAlister worked closely together, chiefly in Cornwall and Devon, taking many of the early glass plate negatives of mining and its associated practices. Which of them took each photograph is not recorded, although often one or the other appears for the purpose of scale in the photographs.

In 1910 a young man named John (Jack) Rhodes joined the Survey as a general assistant. John Rhodes soon became involved with taking photographs, a job which he held until he retired in 1956. During his long career with the Survey Rhodes added almost nine thousand images to the collection, spending much of his time photographing in south-west England. In the early days he would carry his equipment on a donkey or horse and cart, for which he received a daily hay allowance. He was later supplied with a motorcycle

BGS's photographers are based both in Keyworth and Edinburgh, and work chiefly for the core scientific groups within the BGS. This work includes original photography, slide production high magnification photography and digital image manipulation. The NAPG is an established commercial concern and a publications and sales service provides images for a wide range of customers.

A computer database of photographic descriptions enables images from the collection to be located easily through 'key word' searches. The database also allows images to be stored digitally and several thousand photographs have been scanned and stored in this way. The process of digitalisation will continue until every image has been computerised when it is intended that the whole collection will become available for viewing via the Internet.

Archibald Gelkie certainly started something back in 1891!

Above left: *Creswell Gorge, Derbyshire, 1911.*
Above right: *Howden Reservoir, Derbyshire 1904 (first picture in collection).* ***Below:*** *Tomlinson's Brick works, Mansfield, Notts, 1911.*

Meeting the needs of the food retailer

The archetypal grocer is cheerful and friendly, always anxious to please the customer. Now much more than a humble corner shop, Leivers Brothers Limited has not lost sight of these distinctive selling points that helped establish its fame. Its staff still provide a friendly and efficient service, backed by reliable and dependable deliveries. In business since 1880, Leivers Brothers supplies an extensive range of fresh, chilled and frozen foods to independent retail butchers, delicatessens and caterers. Backed by purpose built warehouse and storage facilities, all equipped to European food hygiene and food safety standards, Leivers Brothers continues to offer high quality and wholesome foods to the independent specialist. Keenly priced, the company products provide excellent service to the home market.

Managing director Jeremy Leivers represents the fourth generation of the family business that began when the brothers, Alfred Herbert and Edward Hopkin Leivers, opened a shop on Derby Road. From its position opposite the cathedral, the shop retailed bacon, cheese, butter and cooked meats. Food was imported from all parts of the British Empire. (Only older readers will remember when we had one!) Brokers in Liverpool and London dealt with the handling of the food through the ports. By 1898 a customer base had been established that seemed to grow almost daily. A larger shop in Hockley was added and this became the focal point of the Leivers' excursion into the wholesale trade. There were already about 20 employees, so well and speedily had the business grown. One of these was a certain Henry Smith. He joined the workforce as a junior employee on the princely sum of 17s 6d (87.5p) per week! When he retired in 1953, after 54 years' service, he had risen to the post of managing director and chairman. Both the founding brothers died in the 1920s and a second generation of the family, Edward (known as Mr Eric) Leivers became the chairman.

Above: *An early Christmas advertising promotion.*
Below: *The shop at Derby Road.*

Henry Smith joined the board and he and Mr Eric took the company into a period of steady expansion. Family connections were assured when Henry Smith's son, Harold, joined the firm on the bottom rung in 1931. He worked his way up to managing director and both he and his father put in over 50 years of service to the company. A third generation of the Leivers family went on to sit behind the chairman's desk when Mr Eric's daughter, Joan Morton, assumed the position in 1953.

The company was further guided with the appointment of John Mounteney in 1975. As managing director he built up the firm from one which had experienced modest but steady growth to one which saw rapid expansion and rising profit. He became chairman in 1999.

The wholesale business went from strength to strength and a complete range of fresh provisions was added to complement the traditional business on which Leivers Brothers was founded. The second world war created difficulties because of shortages and rationing. Imported food was in short supply and there was not much in the way of home produce, either. Retail price control meant low profit margins. Strategic changes were made in the 1950s and 1960s. Specialisation in wholesaling became the company's cornerstone and the retail business was dropped. The company moved to its Arnold premises in 1967 to concentrate on fresh foods.

The management at Leivers Brothers has never been afraid to show its human side. A sense of humour is just as important in the business world as anywhere else. The Leivers family still chuckles about a couple of stories from nearly a century ago. In 1911 the company received two claims for damages. A woman in West Bridgford was sent flying from her bicycle when she collided with the company horse and cart. To make matters worse a gentleman of Hyson Green lodged an indignant claim after being bitten by one of the horses. After much complaining and threats of all manner of litigation, both the claimants agreed to settle for £1! That was not much different from Henry Smith's weekly wage of a few years earlier. With a mixture of pragmatism and modernism, Leivers Brothers continues to embrace change as consumers' needs alter. Purchasing from the country's leading food producers, Leivers Brothers' team of experienced professionals provide a service built on a century of knowledge gained in the development of a successful business.

*Above: Deliveries in the late 1930s. **Right:** Leiver's bacon yard preparation area.*

Three generations of personal service

In 1906, two journeymen plumbers, Maurice Cooper and Fred Berry, joined forces to open a business as plumbers and ironmongers. Both had existing premises in the city, Fred Berry at 538 Mansfield Road Sherwood, and Maurice Cooper at Arkwright Street. Both premises had an ironmongers shop, and it takes little imagination to picture the two Edwardian gentlemen in those early days, surrounded by the nails, shovels and buckets which would be the accoutrements of an ironmongers shop of the day. In about 1910, the Arkwright Street shop was closed and a new shop was opened slightly nearer to the city centre, at the corner of St. Stephens Road and Sneinton Hollows. At that time the workshop was transferred to Meadow Lane. Their original trade was as gas fitters; gas lighting was the modern technology of the day, and had become the 'in thing' with householders. At the time a plumber needed to be a glazier and a heating engineer in addition to his own trade of plumbing.

In 1913, however, the partnership was dissolved, Fred Berry keeping his original premises in Mansfield Road and Maurice Cooper taking over the business, which retained its old name of Cooper and Berry. After owning premises at Cutts Factory in Sherwood Street then at Pennycroft Works, Hayward Street, these premises were compulsorily purchased by Nottingham Corporation, who wished to develop the site. The shop at Mansfield Road was owned by the brewery and it had to be transferred to Nottingham Road when the Robin Hood Inn in Mansfield Road was extended. The company eventually moved in 1951 to Central Avenue, New Basford, where they remain today.

Below: Taking a well-earned break in the 1960s.
Bottom: One of the company's wagons in the 1920s.

M E Cooper is mentioned on the list of plumbers who had been registered for efficiency by the Worshipful Company of Plumbers in London, in 1923. In 1938, the company was incorporated, its first directors being Maurice Cooper who acted as chairman, Maurice's sons Ken and Reg Cooper, and George Payne, who had started with the firm as a shop foreman.

Between 1906 and the 1970s, members of the Cooper and Berry Company ran classes in plumbing at the local technical college. Over the years, courses in first year plumbing were taught not only by Maurice Cooper, but also by Reg and Ken Cooper and Frank Browning, a former partner at the company. It is interesting to note that Maurice Cooper's father was also a plumber, and in his later years he also joined the company. As a result there was a time when there were three generations of the Cooper family working for the company at the same time!

Roofing lead and cast iron were the primary raw materials used by the company. Cooper & Berry Ltd also played its part in the war effort, where its experience in metal working was invaluable in the making of metal handles for tanks.

The company which started its existence in Edwardian times as an old fashioned plumbers and ironmongers gradually changed its image to suit the needs of a new generation. In 1962 Chris Bagshaw joined the firm as office junior and learned the trade. The appointment of the young man was a key move, as time would tell....

Cooper and Berry have now become plumbers merchants and instead of selling their own expertise, started to sell their own specialised equipment to other plumbers, a change which they underwent in the 1970s. In spite of this the company still provides prefabricated lead products which are used nationally in the plumbing, building and double glazing trades. Interestingly, the company also provides universities with lead pipes for testing. Another important customer of the company is British Lead Mills of Welwyn Garden City, who are supplied with lead products made in Nottingham. Cooper and Berry also still supply the building trade with items which are made of lead, but its products have been adapted to suit the modern age and it has more important customers than it had in the early days.

The year 2000 saw Chris Bagshaw, who started out as an office junior back in 1962, carry on in the tradition of George Payne, the director who started out as shop foreman, as he purchased the company with his wife, Kathryn.

Chris Bagshaw puts down the company's success to the fact that its sales director and overmen have all trained as hands-on plumbers. Their familiarity with every client's need has helped to give Cooper & Berry the fine reputation they enjoy today. He can be justifiably proud of the company's attention to personal service and customer satisfaction.

Above: *Lead fabrication.*

Climbing the ladder to the top

John and Peter Bratt are members of the third generation of the family business that has developed into one of the country's best established ladder making companies. A fourth generation, Stephen and Peter Jr, already involved in the trade, wait their turn on the bottom rung ready to continue the work their great grandfather began in the 19th century. It was in 1895 that Alfred Bratt made his first set of ladders in a small workshop in Cross Street. His client was a window cleaner. From that modest start Bratt's ladders, now established on the Lenton Industrial Estate, have customers across the country and into Europe, supplying the electrical and communications industries. As well as supplying the 'leg up' for the window cleaning trade, Alfred made barrows and carts for the building trade. The first premises were restricted, being but a yard and a small workshop area. But, old Alfred made a go of it, despite the restrictions on all businesses imposed by the shortages in the first world war. A true craftsman, he cut his ladder rungs from the spokes of large cart wheels. Not for him, of course, the wielding of an electric saw or the use of a lathe. He laid the wheels on a large chopping block and went to work swinging an axe. The stiles (uprights) were cut at a local timber merchants and hand painted.

After the war the business moved to Huntingdon Street, where Alfred was joined by his son, John Alfred (Alf). As was the custom in family trades, the arts and specialisms were passed on from father to son without the need for day release at college or some fancy night school course.

Above left: *Alf Bratt in 1920. He founded the business.* **Below:** *Huntingdon Street in 1930.*

From Huntingdon Street the firm moved to East Street. Here they were in purpose built premises and the old skills had to be adapted to work with the modern machinery of the times. In 1938 the founder died and Alf took over sole control. Almost immediately he had to face the restrictions of the second world war. Timber was in woefully short supply. Fortunately, a contract with Woodhall Duckham Construction Company was arranged. This company built and serviced gasholders. This was government licensed work, but it meant that timber was available, albeit on a quota system.

When peacetime returned A Bratt & Son Ltd began to make inroads into larger business stakes. The next generation of ladder makers came on board when Alf's sons, John and Peter, joined their father. For years the main wood used for the stiles has been Douglas fir. It is imported from Oregon, in the United States. Straight grained and knot free, it is ideal for the job. The rungs are usually cut from ash. All the cutting and turning is done on autolathes and all the work is produced on modern machinery. No painting is carried out on wooden ladders as they are all spray varnished.

Today's market place has ladders that extend, fold and slide. There are trestles, staging and platforms. They can be aluminium or glass fibre, as well as wooden. Two section or three section ladders, combination ladders or steps, the choice is vast. There are particular models for fruit pickers, surveyors and roofers. It is all a far cry from the humble ladder Alfred Bratt made for that window cleaner over 100 years ago.

As A Bratt & Son heads on into these first years of a new millennium, it does so with a firm client base. All the electricity boards, BT, rail companies, local councils and major industry rely on the company's top class product. Unlike a number of its competitors, it sells a kite marked product that conforms to the appropriate British Standard in 95 per cent of its range. In fact, one of Bratt's major selling points is that not only does it conform to the British Standard, it far exceeds it. The company offers a wider and more comprehensive product range than its major competitors. It uses timber that has been specially sourced for its individual use and is the best that is available. This helps Bratt's be a cut above the rest.

Above: *John Alfred Bratt.*
Below: *Bratt's delivery lorry.*

Lighting up Nottingham

Few of those who watched Nottingham's illuminations for the Centenary celebrations in 1949 can have spared much thought for those who actually set up the complicated electrical lighting systems necessary to put on the display. But of course someone had to do the difficult task in order to provide the pleasure experienced by the thousands who celebrated the Centenary.

In fact the work of making sure Nottingham's colourful centenary celebrations went according to plan was undertaken by the local firm of RJ Pickford (Electrical) Ltd. The firm provided all the illuminations on the River Trent Embankment, supplying fairy lights strung from tree to tree along with scenes loaned from Blackpool's Golden Mile. At the same time the firm provided a similar service at the Arboretum, setting up lights, squirrels up trees, rabbits along the ground and other celebratory lighting.

Below: *The company's premises on Randal Street, Hyson Green in a picture dating from the 1950s.*

previously worked as a representative for GEC. That partnership survived until the continuing growth of the business made it necessary to move to new premises at Church Street, Daybrook.

Around that time a significant opportunity arose for the fledgling company: the development of its security business under the trade name of Hornet Alarms. It was not long before the firm's yellow alarm bell covers began appearing all over the city.

Alas not everything was destined to run so smoothly. Misfortune struck the firm when Rolls Royce went into liquidation curtailing the employment of 80 per cent of its work force. The Pickford family decided to sell the electrical contracting arm of the business to Luminaire, a highly successful local light-fitting wholesaler in the city.

The Embankment lights were formally switched on by the familiar figure of the Lord Mayor accompanied by a young lad called Dennis who was in part the son of Harold Jones - Pickford's longest serving employee. It was Harold Jones who was in charge of all the wiring and erecting of the illuminations. Things of course worked perfectly perhaps as a result of Harold Jones' long experience, not the least being when he had been responsible for illuminating Arnot Park celebrating Queen Elizabeth's Coronation on behalf of RJ Pickford.

The firm of RJ Pickford (Electrical) Ltd has recently resettled in new offices and store at Newbourne House, Bulwell but the business has had a varied history and ownership.

The firm's origins go back to 1928 when it began as a shop on Hyson Green

The association with Luminaire lasted only one year however, before the Managing Director at that time, Mr JN Slack acquired the assets and its new offices - by then on Lincoln Street, Basford.

From 1973 onwards the company traded steadily with many well known city companies, local and Government Authorities, Universities and Health Authorities.

During this period a young apprentice was engaged, Mr Ian J Roe, who progressed rapidly to Estimator, Supervisor and later, following the sudden illness of Mr JN Slack - to being the owner and Managing Director.

The firm's origins go back to 1928 when it began life as a shop on Hyson Green. The business was founded, owned and run by a Mr Farrow who owed much of his success to a limited trade mainly working for wealthy customers living in 'The Park' to whom he provided domestic services. The firm's founder, however, also carried out some electrical contracting.

Immediately after the war in 1945 Mr Farrow was joined by Mr Roy Pickford after whom the limited company would take its name. Roy Pickford had

The company has progressed further under Mr Roe's leadership and soon moved to larger premises at Newbourne House in Bulwell where its tight knit workforce is now less like a typical business and more like a family.

Ian Roe runs Pickfords with extremely loyal staff. The notion of the firm as a family is amply demonstrated by the sheer length of time employee's have tended to stay with the firm: at the time of writing a number of employees have over thirty years service.

Above: The premises at Newbourne House, Bulwell.

This is one firm at least which can truthfully say has managed to make light work of making lights work.

Taking the plunge in Nottingham

Did you know that more than 250 million Speedo swimming costumes have been sold world-wide?

Speedo swimming costumes have been manufactured in Nottingham since 1971. Swimmers in the United Kingdom however have been able to buy imported Speedo swimwear, with its distinctive boomerang logo, since 1964 - but the brand is much older even than that.

The early days

Until the 1920s swimming costumes for both men and women were usually full length neck to knee swimsuits in cotton or wool. Some designs for men as well as women included skirts. Older readers will certainly remember wearing swimming trunks or swimming costumes made from cotton or horribly itchy and ill-fitting wool.

Speedo, the world's number one swimwear brand, began life in Sydney Australia in 1928 at the MacRae Knitting Mills which originally manufactured underwear. In that year the name Speedo was

> *Until the 1920s swimming costumes were usually full length neck to knee in cotton or wool*

born, as was the company's first swimsuit, the 'Racerback'. Originally made from silk, the Racerback suit, which featured a high narrow back panel which allowed full shoulder movement, was immediately adopted by world champion swimmers such as Annie Borg which quickly ensured the popularity of the suit and Speedo's position as the word's leading swimwear brand. Silk, though more expensive than cotton, had the advantage of lower water resistance in addition to lightness and strength when worn in competition; all the early swim suits were navy blue.

The actual name 'Speedo' was incidentally suggested by a MacRae Mills employee, a former sea captain named Parsonson, who won £5 for his suggestion of the marketing slogan 'Speed on in your Speedos'.

Finding a niche

Since most swim suits in the 1930s were made of wool or cotton, the silk Speedo Racerback took the

Below: *Swimmers modelling swimsuit styles from the 1920s.*

world's swimming community by storm and continued to dominate the market through the 1930s and 40s. Speedo became a company name only in 1937 when the Speedo Knitting Mills company was formed.

In 1957 Speedo led the way with the world's' first nylon swimsuit which had superior fitting properties to silk and was even lighter in weight. In the 1970s Speedo continued the quest for swimwear excellence with the introduction of its nylon/Lycra swimsuit which is still the world's' most popular swimwear fabric.

The Pentland Group Plc acquired ownership of Speedo International and the Speedo brand in 1991. In 1992 Speedo launched S2000. The suit reduced surface resistance by up to 15 per cent and at the 1992 Barcelona Olympics four world swimming records were broken and seven gold medals were won by swimmers wearing the S2000 suit.

World beaters
In 1996 Speedo launched its Aquablade range with 23 per cent lower surface resistance than conventional fabrics. At the Atlanta Olympics in 1996 three out of four world swimming records were broken by swimmers wearing Aquablade costumes - and 89 per cent of medals won at the World Swimming Championships held in Hong Kong in 1999 were awarded to competitors wearing Speedo swimwear.

2000 saw the launch of the FAST.SKIN. Speedo FAST.SKIN has been developed using biomimetics: the extraction of good design from nature. The fabric is based on a sharks skin, it mimics the V-shaped ridges and denticles allowing the body to slip through the water more smoothly. Fabric tests

show that FAST.SKIN has a 3 per cent lower surface resistance than Aquablade.

As might be expected in a company with such a high profile Speedo sponsors many competitions and individuals: the firm has sponsored such events as the 'Speedo British Grand Prix' and the 'Speedo Leagues'; it can also boast an elite squad of British swimmers sponsored by the brand including James Hickman, Mark Foster, Grahame Smith, Karen Pickering and Katy Sexton.

Today the Speedo International company, based at Ascot Road's Bobbers Mill, is, in addition to being the world's number one brand of swimwear, embracing all products associated with water activities. That range of products now includes the familiar swim hats and goggles as well as the less familiar 'kickboards' and sports towels. Additionally Speedo is also producing Triathlon, Aquatic Fitness and Beach Volleyball products and is working with top athletes in each of these fields. For example Spencer Smith of Great Britain, the double World Triathlon champion, and Karch Kiraly of the USA, the world's leading Beach Volleyball player are both sponsored by Speedo.

And today...
The firm's product range continues to increase and now includes shoes, bags and a variety of other swimming related equipment. And, in a curious rerun of its own history, Speedo now also manufactures men's and women's underwear, some of which is 95 per cent cotton - like the boomerang on its logo the company has returned to its point of origin!

Top: *An aerial view of the premises 20 years ago.*

Plumbing the heights

The firm of FG Skerritt Ltd will have touched the lives of many Nottingham residents in the century or more of its existence. The Skerritt story began in 1899 when local plumber Francis (Frank) Greenfield Skerritt established his plumbing firm from his home at 33 Ebury Road, Carrington - the address from which the business would continue to be run until 1985!

ESTABLISHED 1899

F. G. Skerritt Limited

SKERRITT

DIRECTORS:
F. G. SKERRITT, R.P., M.I.P.
MARK SKERRITT, A.M.I.MECH.E., A.M.I.H.V.E.
K. SKERRITT: SECRETARY:

33, Ebury Road
NOTTINGHAM
PHONES: 62551/2

HEATING, VENTILATING & ELECTRICAL ENGINEERS

Frank Skerritt was the son of a prominent Nottingham plumber Tommy Skerritt who was reputedly less than keen to grant his newly qualified son, aged twenty-one, a man's share of the family business. So Frank set up on his own.

Business grew steadily. Frank Skerritt formed the Nottingham Electric Welding Company which in 1904 won the contract to weld the tram lines over the Trent Bridge. That same year the business took on its first employee: a thirteen year old apprentice named Fred Wilcox who was to remain with the firm for a record sixty three years before retiring in 1967.

The business became a limited company in 1919 taking on ever larger contracts. By the 1920s many plumbing firms had begun taking on electrical work. Skerritt was no exception, carrying out its first combined plumbing and electrical contract on Middleton Boulevard in 1924.

By 1930 it was decided that the best way to expand was to move into the far more profitable heating and ventilation business. Frank Skerritt's son Mark, a young man who, in common with his two sisters, had actually been born at the company headquarters in Ebury Road trained in the heating field and went to the University of Nottingham to study electrical engineering. Mark joined his father in 1934.

Below: *No 33 Ebury Road which was once the home of the Skerritt family. As the company expanded Mark Skerritt had the extension on the left of the picture made into an office for himself and the company eventually acquired the property next door to extend the office space, making the two houses into one.*

The company consolidated its position in the war years, being awarded many contracts to provide the lead roofs for aircraft hangars. By 1945 the firm was financially sound and in a position to attack the post war market. With the relaxation of building controls in 1953 the firm, now led by Mark Skerritt, moved into its boom years; in the 1960s the firm was employing over 200 people. The World Cup year of 1966 however was tinged with sadness at Skerritt when the company's founder Frank Skerritt died at the grand age of 87.

By that time 85 per cent of Skerritt's business was 'design and build' - mainly housing and schools. By 1969 the firm was achieving 100 house completions per week and 20 schools per year. Between 1955 and 1971 Skerritt designed and completed every new school built in Lancashire and a vast number of schools for the Catholic Diocese; between 1961 and 1971 it was involved in the design, installation and completion of 9,500 timber frame houses.

By the 1960s the firm was employing over 200 people

The Skerritt family sold the business to Galliford in 1968 which then entered a new phase as a subsidiary company. In 1980 Bernard Gregg was appointed managing director holding that post until the firm's centenary year, 1999.

The company remained part of Galliford until the early 1980s during which time it continued to win large contracts. In 1983 Galliford decide to sell Skerritt to its current owner the Melton Medes Group. Meanwhile Skerritt was maintaining a net profit level on turnover of five to seven per cent and increasing turnover by 10 to 15 per cent per annum.

At the time of the sale to Melton Medes most of the contracts Skerritt was carrying out were in excess of a million pounds, several worth more then two million. But Skerritt was shifting away from housing and into more technical fields. Perhaps symbolically the mid 1980s saw the firm move from its old offices to its present location at 24 Union Road, Nottingham.

The early 1990s economic recession hit the construction industry hard. Skerritt did not escape unscathed when three of its best customers, representing 50 per cent of turnover went into liquidation.

Having to find new markets Skerritt moved on to water engineering. It also moved into the field of prefabricated prison buildings, schools and hotels.

Today Skerritt maintains its long standing relationships with most government departments in particular the Home Office and Ministry of Defence.

Following the retirement of Bernard Gregg in 1999 the company is now headed by Les Francis who is committed to continuing the traditions of Skerritt whilst introducing innovations to ensure a future for Skerritt as prosperous as its past.

Above: *Skerritt's current premises to which the company moved in the mid 1980s.*

Half a century in print

The dawn of the new millennium saw one of Nottingham's best known printing firms celebrate its fiftieth year in business.

Planned Print Limited, trading under the name of Progressive Printers (Nottingham), has its roots in a typical small letterpress printing firm formed in 1950 by a small team of printers led by Cecil John Henry Griffin. The company has grown steadily over the years until it now offers a totally comprehensive service, able to provide everything from photography, design and origination through to computerised film and plate making, litho printing, finishing, binding and final delivery. The company's recent period of growth has been largely under the guidance of EJ 'Ted' Shotton whose career with the company goes back to 1955.

The company was originally based in 2,000 sq ft of space rented from the Woolston Book Company in Gamble Street off Alfreton Road, premises which later became John Menzies. Those original premises housed three 'Heidelberg' platens and one Crown-size 'Glockner'. The gradual change from letterpress to litho began in the late 1960s with an investment of £900 in a second hand A3 'Rotaprint' machine, quickly followed by another. By which time the company had moved a few hundred yards to an old mill in Ayr Street which gave the company 3,000 sq ft of space spread over two floors.

In the early 1970s Progressive Printers entered the A2 market acquiring second-hand, a 'Solna 124' and '224'. By the mid 70s C J H Griffin, then chairman and the last of the founder directors, retired and Mr Shotton became managing director. Within a few years another move to larger premises became imperative and in 1980 the company purchased a factory at Westbury Road, Basford which provided 6,000 sq ft of space.

Within a year the printing capacity of the new factory was doubled through the addition of two more 'Solna 425s' bringing the total number to four. At the same time a further £40,000 was spent on air-conditioning the whole factory - priority being given to the machine room, not only to ensure the stability of the ink and water mixtures, but also to make working conditions more comfortable.

Above: *Mr Shotton, Managing Director.*
Below: *An early company celebration.*

the Orkneys and Cornwall. The remaining 60 per cent of turnover being made up of a wide range of brochures, leaflets, promotional and advertising material supplied to local authorities, universities, and the business community.

At the end of the 1980s the company purchased its present premises also on Westbury Road, Basford, previously used as the Nottingham base for Spicer Cowen paper merchants. This provides Progressive with over 12,000 sq ft on one floor and an ideal layout for its Komori Lithrone presses and recently re-equipped finishing department.

After celebrating the first fifty years in business Nottingham's Progressive Printers is now setting its sights on celebrating its centenary in 2050!

Established in ideal working conditions, the 1980s saw the company consolidating its existing services and introducing new ones. On the print side the second-hand 'Solnas' were gradually replaced with a complete range of presses starting in 1983 with two four-colour 'Komori Sprints' followed by a two-colour 'Sprint' in 1985 and a single-colour in 1986 - all sharing the same plate size for optimum flexibility and representing a financial commitment of over £500,000.

By this time about 40 per cent of Progressive's workload was long-run work for the wholesaling and catering trades where the firm frequently produced several hundred thousand food or confectionery catalogues for wholesalers as far apart as

Top: *Westbury Road, the premises today.*
Above: *Ayr Street, home to the company from the late 1960s until 1980.*
Right: *Gamble Street, the beginning.*

A photograph of wartime evacuees from the South East arriving in a Nottinghamshire village

Acknowledgments

The Nottingham Post Group Limited

Nottingham City Council: Leisure and Community Services: Central Library, and particularly Mrs Dorothy Ritchie of the Local Studies Library

Several local photographers and their descendants - especially Mr JG Atkins, Mr W Spencer, Mr Frank Stevenson and Mrs May Sentance

Geoffrey Oldfield

Thanks are also due to Margaret Wakefield who penned the editorial text and Steve Ainsworth for his copywriting skills